Burst Gibson

By Jay Scott and Vic Da Pra

SunBurst Les Paul

ISBN 1-57424-203-2

SAN-683-8022

P.O. Box 17878 - Anaheim Hills, CA 92817

Table of Contents

Aknowledgements

The authors wish to thank the following businesses and individuals without those participation this book would have been less complete:

Tom Wittrock, Third Eye Music
Richie Frieman, We Buy Guitars
Kosta Kovachev
Albert Molinaro
Revised Layout: **Dave Collins**

Gary Winterflood
Mark Quinton
Scott Chinery
Rudy Pensa

Scott Frielich, Top Shelf Music
Chelsea Second Hand Guitars
Art Atwood

Authors

Vic DaPra has always been an intergral part of the music scene in the Pittsburgh, PA area. A lifelong devotee of the guitar about which he would eventually co-author two books, Vic received his first 'burst as a gift in the early 1970s; it cost a then-outrageous $1600. Since that time he has owned many examples of what has become a pre-eminent American collectible. Along with partner Tim Matyas, he opened the Guitar Gallery in Canonsburg, PA in 1985, preferring Gibson Historic Les Paul reissues and other high quality six-strings.

Jay Scott is a Jesuit-educated throwback whose publications include *The Guitars of the Fred Gretsch Company*, *'50s Cool: Kay Guitars*, *Sunburst Alley* and the first edition of this book as well as dozens of articles for such periodicals as *Guitar World* and *20th Century Guitar* magazines. His life has been notably unremarkable and unproductive, save for the generation of his glorious, albeit autistic, son Gianni Lux Amlfi-Scognetti Scott, himself a published author and illustrator of two books, *Playing Games* and *From Pumpkin Seed To Pumpkin Pie* (Parker Publishing), and the few aforementioned sporadic insights.

This revitalized version of our paradigmatic Sunburst book is lovingly dedicated to my co-author Vic DaPra whose implaceable goading and cajoling inevitably led to my revising this edition. If I had a nickel for every time Vic would, you'll excuse the expression, fan the flames of my interest in it's revision using Gerard Manley Hopkins' famous finishing couplet from "The Windhover" "... And blue bleak embers, ah my dear, fall, gall themselves and gash gold vermillion" , I'd have enough money to buy an original 'burst. Here's to the once-and-future Pharoah of Flame!!

To Steve DiVenuta, the office tiger, who coalesced all our efforts to bring this project to - I use the word loosely - fruition.

To Ron Middlebrook, Centerstream Publishing

Finally and most gratefully to Larry and Jim Acunto of *20th Century Guitar* magazine/ Seventh String Press - for 20 years of friendship and association and for graciously and generously releasing the copyright on this book thereby allowing yet another guitar book to be foisted on the already - overwhelmed, guitar-related public.

Jay Scott

Preface

"Since the first publication of this book 'til today, the sunburst has continued to inspire me and new generations of musicians. Thank you, Les."

- James Patrick Page

Jimmy Page live at the Filmore East, NewYork City, May 1969.
(James Acunto)

"It was 1974. My group The Butts Band was playing a gig in Boston. We were co-billed with the Ann Peebles Group. The guitar player was a guy appropriately named Robert Johnson. One day I noticed his guitar; it was unlike anything I had ever seen. I had always used Gibsons, SGs, Les Pauls, etc., but this one was something else. It was a 1960 Les Paul cherry sunburst with flames from hell. It was so well balanced and played so nice, I'd never seen anything so beautiful before or after. He wanted $3000 for it. I thought he was crazy. $3000 for a used guitar?

There was no such thing as vintage instruments in those days. I've been kicking myself ever since. Anyway, five years ago, my friend Al Jackson, guitar and golf enthusiast, introduced me to Dave Belzer and Drew Berlin, the famous "Burst Brothers" at the Guitar Center. They had come across a sunburst LP just over eight pounds, it is one of the lightest I've ever seen (this is a good thing). Nice flames, good color, but the neck is the best part. Those '60 necks were the best in my opinion. So I finally have my burst! Now allowing for inflation and all that, my new guitar, christened Kriegerburst by Al Jackson, is still a good deal. Supposedly it's tripled in value in five years. Not that I would ever sell it!"

-Robby Krieger

Introduction

Certainly, the Gibson Les Paul "sunburst" Standard has become the singularly most desirable and collectable electric guitar ever made. Its repute and value are virtually common knowledge and its marque has almost become a household name. Its devotees invest mortgage-size sums into individual examples and kings' ransoms into life-long collections of the blue-chip, investable guitar, and lovingly lavish nicknames on the objects of their affection in a kind of dementia author Richard Smith has referred to a sunburst psychosis.

But it wasn't always so. despite contemporary sunburst enthusiasts' need to elevate the instrument to the sanctum sanctorum, sound historical perspective and an insight into corporate reasoning insinuates that the company viewed the new 1958 model askance, as a bit of a pariah, a second-rate guitar, a marketing and design compromise. contemporary hysteria and emotion aside, the sunburst Standard followed a Les Paul goldtop sales slide that had decreased Les Paul model production 200% by the mid-fifties. Obviously, Gibson reasoned correctly, it was time for a change. But how to shore up slumping sales of the company's second-best solidbody? The answer was reasonable - and typical - for a traditional firm like Gibson: put a flamed maple top with a sunburst finish on the model. In every sense this was a retrogression for the Les Paul model, and Gibson knew it. the gold-finished Les Paul had been a stretch for the company, a bold stroke of color and daring for the stodgy, sunburst-and-natural-finish-oriented manufacturer. So, when the corporate decision was made to return to the sunburst finish, it was, in a very real sense, a de-evolution, a step backwards. One even gets the impression of boardroom exasperation and resignation, of not knowing what to do next with the damn model. combined with the fact that the standard was relatively cheap -- the Super 400, L-5, Byrdland, ES-350, the higher line thinlines and other were the company's heavy hitters; even the Les Paul Custom cost almost twice as much as the Standard -- a feeling of near-indifference emerges: "Well, the goldtop was good for us for a few years but sales are in the toilet now. So let's go back to the look that got us where we are; we'll make the thing look like a baby L-5 or Super 400, put a sunburst finish on it since Fender seems to be doing okay with their Stratocaster, price it cheap and pitch it as a second instrument for the pro who doesn't want to take his L-5 to the gig or to the guy who wants to sit home and play and won't feel bad about laying out 250 bucks for a guitar that sort of looks like our good stuff. . . .and see if it flies."

No, it didn't. And for one reason or another (primarily poor sales) the guitar was removed from the line at the end of 1960 after an unremarkable 2 1/2 years in Gibson's - another Gibson solidbody debacle, certainly not of the magnitude of Gibson's BIG faux pas, the Korina series, but surely nothing to write home to Kalamazoo about.

With such inauspicious beginnings, even the most devout 'burst worshippers must admit, the Standard was not a glowing success. . . . and it seems Gibson knew it wasn't going to be. Or else how does one explain the almost casual disregard the company showed in matching curly maple tops on many of the Standards? Or the fact that 75% of all Standards do not have dramatic figure in their maple caps . . . or little or no figure at all? Or the reason such a light-fugitive (light sensitive) red aniline dye was used for the cherry sunburst when Gibson *knew* it was going to fade and was well aware of the availability of better, more durable, more light-fast, more *costly* dyes? (Michael Dresdner, "Restoration Clinic," *Vintage Guitar Bulletin,* Vol 3 No. 1, Jan., 1984).

The answer to all these rhetorical questions is obvious. But as all of us have so often learned in the dominion of the classic American guitar yesterday's debacle sometimes turns into today's treasure; the past's pariah reappears as the present's avatar. In the case of the 1958-'60 Les Paul Standard, a late-'50's middle-of-the-road yawner emerges as the turn-of-the-century Holy Grail. The prodigal son has returned home a saint.

Prologue

In preparing the revisions and additions for this resuscitated edition of our Sunburst book, my co-author, Vic DaPra and I had numerous conversations about content, of course, but eventually virtually all our talks edged into a more – how shall I say this – philosophical realm. More precisely, we invariably came to discuss, somewhat sadly, somewhat bemusedly, the astronomical prices that particular examples of the guitar had achieved over the past few years. 'Bursts have skyrocketed in value from low-five-figure collectibles to six-figure untouchables, sometimes commanding prices in excess of $200,000. affordable only by millionaires. 'Burst ownership has become the province of high-profile authors and their publishers, prominent actors, doctors and lawyers…entrepreneurial titans, not musicians. Vic would chuckle that many of the original proponents of the model couldn't begin to afford one now.

This begs the obvious question, then: what precisely are we dealing with here…now…precisely? Is this a musical instrument or a cultural icon? Apparently, its very nature has changed along with its raison d'être. The days when dirty white boys blared jungle music on these hammers of the gods and in so doing busted down all kinds of walls have clearly past; a 'burst is as much a guitar nowadays as a Louis Quatorze table is an eating platform. Sure, occasionally still, some atavistic giant like Slash, Joe Perry, Joe Walsh or Billy Gibbons has the balls to step center-stage and burn on an original sunburst Les Paul like the old days unafraid he might fracture a headstock and so ruin his investment. But what has become painfully evident is that the nature of the beast, the 'burst's essence, has changed. Indisputably, the epoch of 'burst-as-bauble is upon us. The sunburst-finished 1958-1960 Les Paul Model/Les Paul Standard is now the domain of the super-rich; Peter Green need not apply.

What New York City-based, sunburst maven Doug Myer of Dan Courtenay's Chelsea Guitars so aptly wrote about Slash, the last-ever, 'burst welding, guitar god, several years ago now seems equally apropos to the instrument he proffered: after he bashed his way through the temple doors with his flametops, the closed behind him forever.

Jay Scott
(I can't believe I'm still in) Rochester, New York, 2005

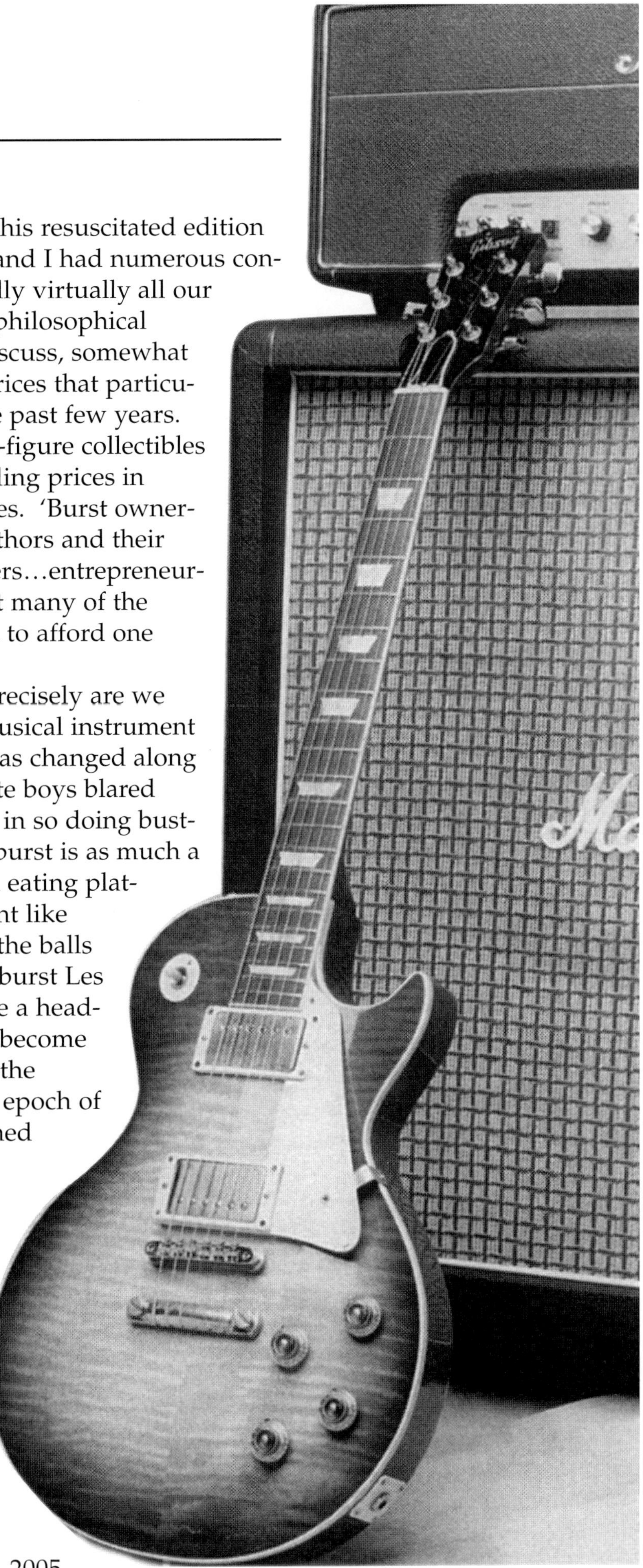

1959 Standard/E Clark. Photo W. Draffen

1958's

1958 & 1959

May be the most innovative years of the post-World War II era. For some reason, the aesthetics of the early postwar period and modern technology coalesced during these formative years. just as 1939 may arguably be considered the most inspired year of the prewar era, 1958 and 1959 are, in retrospect, the artistic and functional linch-pin of the modern epoch. Witness a society brimming with effusive color schemes and design ideas on interior and exterior design, in architecture, on automobiles, etc.

And these two years were seminal for American guitar manufacturers, too: 3-color sunburst finishes and rosewood fingerboards on Fender Strats and the Filter'Tron pickup and Project-O-Sonic stereo sound on gretsch guitars, among others. Of course, Gibson did its part in these prototypic years by introducing its Thinline series, stereo-varitone and a trio of abortive yet inspired Korina solidbodies.

However, with all this modernity swirling around, the Gibson company, true to its tradition-conscious heritage, took a major step . . . backward; the Kalamazoo-based industry leader made a modest yet unmistakable retro modification in its second-most-expensive solidbody guitar: it put a sunburst-finished, maple top on it to replace the gold-painted one that had graced the Les Paul Model since its inception in 1952. Why? To make the little solidbody attractive to the jazz guitar-playing market; the front of the Standard looked like the back of an L-5 or a Super 400. The decision was an attempt to draw the company's major player-share, the jazz guitarist, into the expensive solidbody market via a move back to Gibson's time-honored, traditional look. The standard was a down-sized, solidbody version of a Gibson jazz guitar right down to its archtop-inspired, contoured, single-cutaway body shape. At its debut price of $247.50, furthermore, the sunburst Standard offered the semi-professional musician or the armchair Mickey Backer an attractive, affordable package to play around the shanty at volume 2.

Some sunburst Les Paul Standards may have been produced in the very high 8-4000 serial number range but the earliest number that can be inferred from existing sample is 8-5000

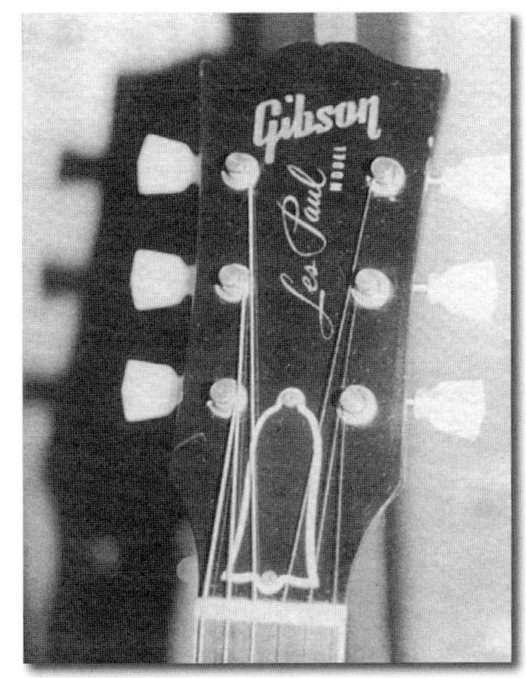

The headstock of a Les Paul Model goldtop from 1957. Note the position and script of the Gibson logo.

The yellow, inked-on serial number from a unique 1959 goldtop Les Paul Model with PAFs and very dark, tobacco-brown back, sides and neck.

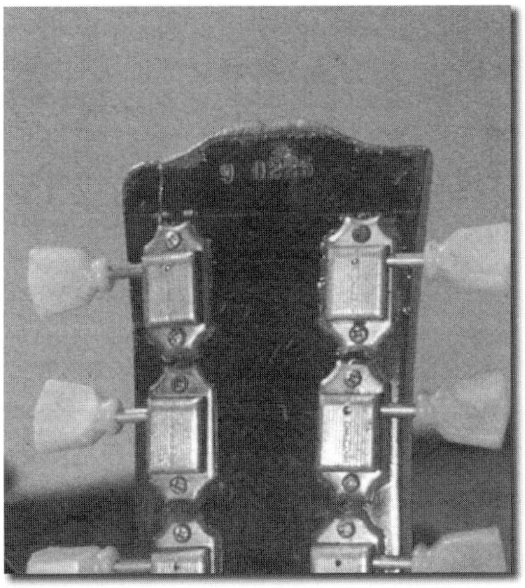

Nobody plays a song like old Buck and leave it to industry mainstay Buck Sulcer to uncover one of the earliest, documented sunburst Les Paul Standards, serial number **8-5325**. 'Bursts began to appear at about serial number 8-5000 in the latter part of 1958, probably I bit later in the year than mid-'58 as has been usually reported by most chroniclers.

Of the four incarnations of the Les Paul Model that preceded the 1958 sunburst Les Paul Standard, this is the last - an early 1958 Les Paul model with a gold-painted top over a curly maple cap, stop tailpiece and tune-o-matic ABR-1 bridge and Patent Applied For humbucking pickups. This variation also appeared in 1957. '57 and '58 goldtop Les Paul models arbitrarily have natural mahogany back, sides and necks or dark-brown back, sides and neck. The former have their serial numbers inked-on in black while the "dark backs" have a yellow, inked-on number. An occasional '57 or '58 PAF goldtop does not have a maple cap over the one-piece mahogany body but instead has a solid-mahogany body, probably intended for the all-mahogany top-of-the-line solidbody Custom model. There seems to be no correlation between the appearance of the maple cap or the dark or light body finish vis-a-vis the year of production.

Mary Ford's 1958 goldtop has ES-295-style, stencilled, gold leaves on the pick-guard and the custom armrest. *(Al Romano/Richie Friedman)*

A trio of 1958 Les Paul Standards demonstrates the part of the range of colors that were available in the pre-sunburst era. From left: a Custom-like, black Standard with nickel hardware, Mary Ford's PAF goldtop and a typical sunburst LP Standard.
(Al Romano/Richie Friedman)

1958-1960 Sunburst Les Paul

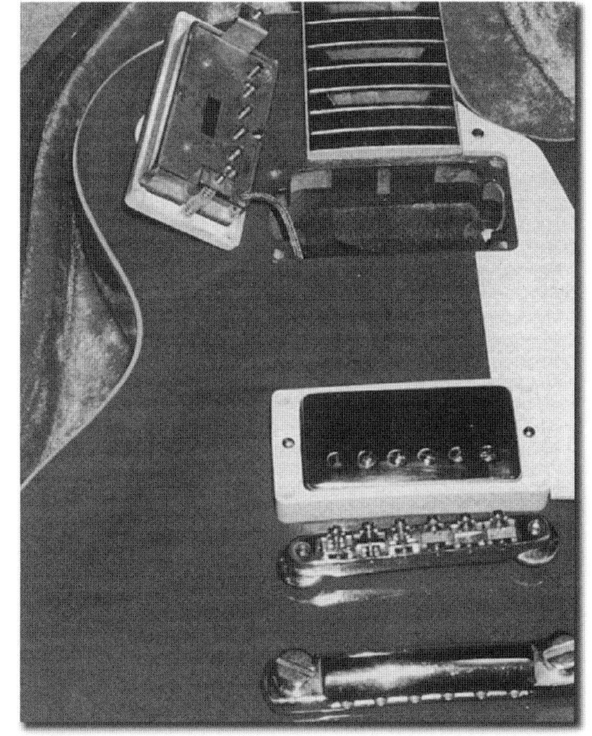

The Standard's 7/16 inch thick maple cap isclearly visible in this photo. Note the typicalhumbucker routing, the neck-body joint, the labeled PAF.

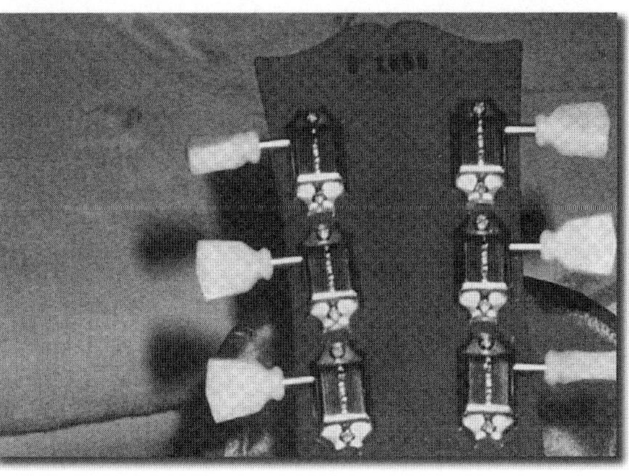

A 1958 inked-on serial number

Sweet Cherry: Ron David's cherry-red finished 1958 Standard, serial number **8-1689**, was issued several thousand serial numbers before the first sunburst Standard appeared.

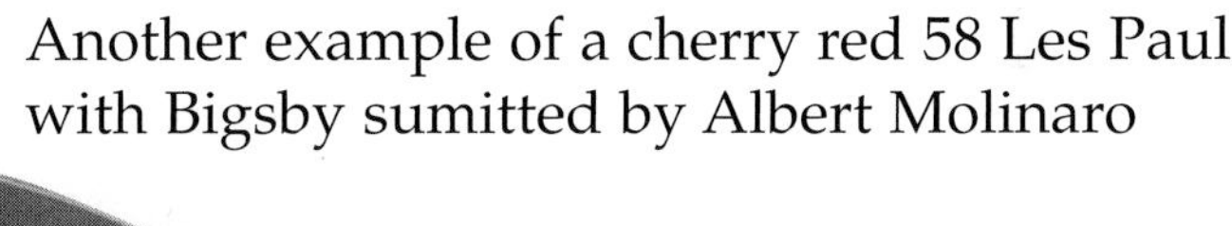

Another example of a cherry red 58 Les Paul with Bigsby sumitted by Albert Molinaro

Serial #number **8-5388**, 1958; The top looks like the mirror image of #8-5386 with its random, irregular squiggles of curl and almost invisible seam. The finish has strong, red color remaining and is warmly translucent demonstrating the wavy figure underneath. There can be no doubt that 8-388 came from the same billet of flamed maple as #8-5386. All that remains is to find **#8-5387**

Serial number **8-5386**, 1958, very early in the sunburst production run of 1958. The guitar's top squiggle curl and shatters of figure all over its profusely-figured top. From some angles it appears that this 'burst has a one-piece top. It doesn't; original one-piece top, 3-piece top or off-center tops do not exist. All sunburst Les Paul Standards have 2-piece, centerseam tops.

Serial #**8-5346**, 1958, left, and another '58 show figure commonly misdescribed as birdseye maple. It is correctly referred to as blister, pock or measle maple and features dime-size, 3-dimensional circles of figure. Although both sides of the centerseam top of #8-5436 are from the same flitch of figured maple, the top is not bookmatched. In fact, it is the rare 'burst that displays true. bookmatching in its top. The other Standard bears similar blister-maple figure on the treble side of the top but the darker, bass side is from a completely unrelated piece of wood.

Serial number **8-5418**, 1958. Note that the irregular figure with arching medullary grain, which runs perpendicular to the flame, hints at bookmatching. The guitar has translucent, wine-red color remaining in its top finish. *(Ron Proler)*

Almost-opaque, cherry-red finish, more like 1960's color than '58 or '59's, covers the lightly-figured top of serial number **8-5495**, 1958. *(Tim Matyas)*

Two shots of a '58 with evenly-distributed bands of short, regular flame all over the top which has remained strong, almost-opaque, cherry-red color. Note the heavy lines of medullary grain running perpendicular to the flame on the switch side.
(Gary Winterflood)

Serial number **8-5803**, 1958 has a lightly-figured, unmatched top whose red aniline has undergone a typical '58-'59 fade. The resulting hue is a transparent, green-brown, light ice-tea color. The bottom '58 has a similar, pale, top finish remaining over broader, nicely-matched ribbon curl. *(Kosta)*

"Floor flame" highlights the top of this unfaded '58. The facetious, somewhat derisive description of a lightly-figured top means that the 'burst must be laid down on the floor and then viewed from a number of angles to see any figuring in the top at all. Note the swirling medullary grain flowing opposite the light, curly figure.

Another '58 with a very active top.

Beautiful, deep, strong, cherry color remains in the top finish of Ron David's '58 'burst serial number 8-6730. The tight pin-stripe curl is almost bookmatched and is the preferred type of curl among many cognoscenti.

Wide swatches of faint, irregular ribbon-curl glisten under translucent cherry-red on this '58 Standard. Note the blank area on the toggle side of the top devoid of any figure whatsoever.

Feel like making love? Mick Ralphs couldn't get enough of this fiercely flamey '58 played on many of Bad Company's classic songs. Captain Crunch's signature sound -- fat, single-string riffs, chunky, ringing, distorted, midrange chords and overdriven, blown speakers -- is the unmistakable timbre and legacy of a classic sunburst. If first position A's and E's barreling through PAFs doesn't make the hair stand up on the back of your neck, you're reading the wrong book, pal. Now, why would anybody pay 25 grand to get that sound? And what about Ralphs? If you listen to the wind you can still hear him play. The guitar was once owned by Gil Southworth of Southworth Guitars, one of the premier dealers of not only sunburst Standards but a broad array of classic American guitars. *(Joe Steffanini)*

Quartet of 59's with Tags

Gibson issued information sheets, pamphlets and tags with the purchase of every new Les Paul Standard including one with the model's name and serial number. Even this paper esoterics has become big medicine on the vintage guitar market and a full set of 'burst tags can fetch $1000 or more. Being well-aware of the light-fugitive (light-sensitive) dyes it was using for the cherry-sunburst, top color of the Standard, the company began issuing its "Mr. Dealer" tag, which cautioned the franchise dealer to keep his Standards out of the store window lest fading occur, in mid-1959.

FOR TOP PERFORMANCE OF YOUR NEW GIBSON

Professionals Attention

This guitar has been adjusted for professional usage (light pick action) which enables the guitarist to fully develop and use his technique, If you use a hard stroke and do not wish to change to a light pick action, raise the bridge slightly to eliminate string rattle. We advise the user of ... strings for low action settings.

Gibson, Inc.

Mr. Dealer:

In order to preserve the delicate coloring of this beautiful Gibson instrument, avoid displaying in show windows where it will be subject to direct or excessive sunrays.

INSTRUCTIONS

TUNE-O-MATIC BRIDGE*

What it does:

Makes it possible to tune your guitar to perfect accuracy on each individual string, at the bridge.

Permits precise adjustment for intonation, regardless of string gauge.

Saddles can be reversed individually, for full range of tuning.

Easily raised or lowered to suit individual preference for solid or feather touch action.

Makes possible longer sustained tones, and increases the playing life of each string.

Allows precise adjustment of each string even under full tension.

Reduces distortion caused by imperfect intonation.

Adds to the beauty and appearance of your guitar.

How to install:

1. Remove old bridge and place Tune-O-Matic bridge in same relative position on guitar.
2. Be sure to have the individual saddle adjusting screw heads towards the fingerboard.
3. Tighten the individual strings to approximately correct pitch.
4. Adjust action height with the thumb nuts in the usual manner. The action height may vary with instruments and players.
5. Now tune the guitar to perfect pitch.
6. For fine tuning, pluck the harmonic at the 12th fret, and then depress the same string to produce the true octave. If the harmonic is sharp, turn the screw for that string counterclockwise until the octaves match. If the harmonic is flat, turn the screw clockwise.
7. Repeat No. 6 for each of the other strings.
8. If you prefer you may notch the saddle top very lightly with the edge of a file.
9. If necessary to remove or change saddles, snap out by pushing on the screw head with your thumb.

Your Tune-O-Matic bridge is precision made of finest materials and with reasonable care should give you a lifetime of trouble-free service.

Product of

GIBSON, INC.
Kalamazoo, Michigan

*Patent Pending

*HUMBUCKING PICKUP ADJUSTMENTS

This guitar has been carefully adjusted by Gibson technicians to provide maximum efficiency and tonal quality.

Should you alter the action height by raising or lowering the bridge or changing the gauge of strings, you must readjust the height of the pickup. Ample adjustment has been provided and can be accomplished by following the simple instructions with Figures 1 and 2.

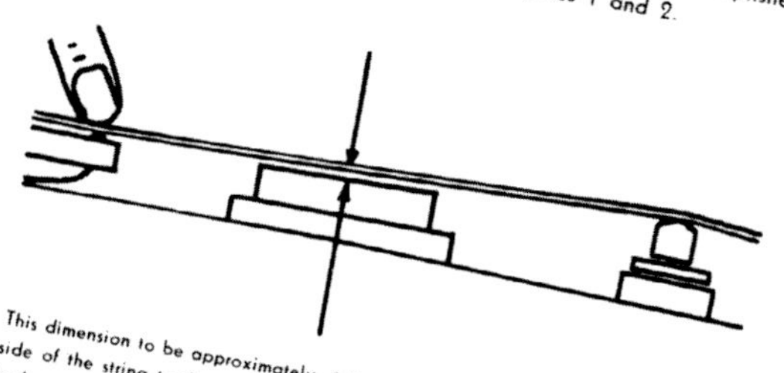

This dimension to be approximately 1/16 from the underside of the string to the top of the pickup when the string is depressed at the last fret of the fingerboard. To raise or lower the entire pickup unit turn the height adjusting screws.

FIG.1

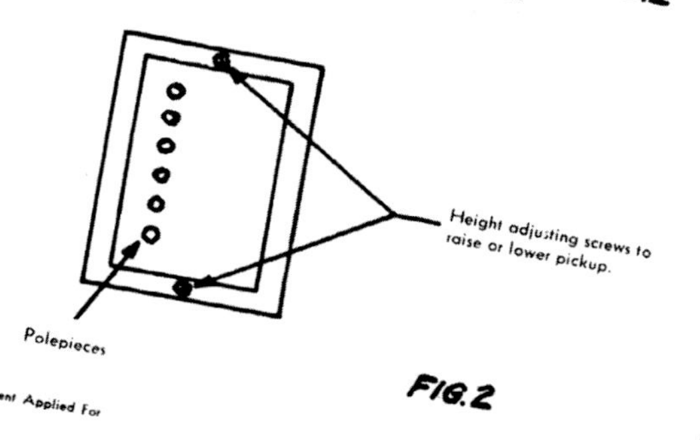

FIG.2

*Patent Applied For

1959

Tradition to 1959

The change to cherry sunburst finish on the Les Paul model was first noted in the Gibson Gazette of December 1958 (Andre Duchossoir, Gibson Electrics, Mediapresse) and the newly-named Standard made its first appearance in production in the latter part of that year at approximate serial number 8-5000 Early-1959's version was identical to its '58 forebear. However, at approximate serial number 9-0600, early in the '59 run of sunbursts, two modifications in the model coincidentally occurred. Virtually undetectable and probably trivial to the guitars' creators, the two specification changes are of such importance to contemporary 'burst aficionados as to make '59's version the desired, de rigueur type.

First, a slightly wire fret wire was introduced to replace the thin frets that had been used on the Les Paul model since its inception in 1952. The wider fret allows strings to be more easily pulled up a step or two for blues and rock styles and allows the bend to be better held and vibratoed. When combined with the slight thinning of the neck's depth in 1959 from the slightly chunkier, '58 contour, optimum neck dimensions and feel had been achieved.

Moreover, and al least as significant, white coil forms, the bobbins around which the 42-gauge wire is wrapped in Patent Applied For humbuckers. began to appear about serial number 9-0600. Because of a lack of black, carbon-based pigment, which had given the uncovered pickup its characteristic color, the pounding heartbeat of the 'burst began to burn white-hot at about this time; by serial number range 9-1000 or 9-1100 white bobbins had begun to predominate in PAFs as zebra and double-whites until the latter part of 1960.

1959's serial number 9-0297 occurred early in the '59 run. The guitar has thin frets like a '58. Its plain top demonstrates almost no figure and has little color remaining except near the switch and on the cutaway. It has double-black PAFs under its nickel covers. (Mark Quinton)

Serial number **9-0341**was produced early in 1959's production run of Standards. This beautiful example has deep, regular flame evenly distributed over both halves of the nicely-matched maple cap. The guitars finish is completely faded to a glowing honey color. Sunbursts that have had their red-aniline color fade completely are referred to as "unbursts." The light-fugitive dyes used for the red color were not very light-fast and faded significantly when exposed to sunlight. . .even though Gibson knew it, they chose not to use costlier, less light-sensitive dyes on the 'burst until mid-1960. #9-0341 has thin frets and double-back-coil PAFs.

Serial number **9-0367**, 1959. The bass side of the maple top has nice, light flame while the treble side is plain. Not only, so it would seem do consecutive-number sunbursts occasionally have dissimilar, maple tops but the same 'burst can have its cap thrown together using two unrelated pieces of wood.

Serial number **9-0368**, 1959, is heavily faded just like its predecessor #9-0367. However, it has very light , nearly invisible pinstripe-curl in the top with dark flecks of mineral. Its top is nothing like that of #9-0367. *(Mark Quinton)*

The headstock of a 1959 sunburst les Paul Standard. Note the white-bordered, bell-shaped truss rod cover and the position of the Gibson logo.

Robert Johnson –no, not the dead bluesman, silly– is a Memphis-based, blues rocker extraordinaire who was up for Mick Taylor's spot in the Stones' cuz he was funky as you wanna be. The 'burst he used with John Entwistle's Ox, and on the Rolling Stones' *Black and Blue* album eventually wound up in Tom Wittrock's collection. Serial number **9-0592**, 1959, has an exquisite, virtually-bookmatched, thick-ribbon-curl top which has completely faded to a consistent honey-amber. The 3-dimensional stripes of ribbon form upward chevrons on this exceedingly bad unburst. The double-white-bobbin PAFs are not original in this instrument, however.

The next consecutive serial number from the Johnson-Wittrock stunner is the author's serial number **9-0593**, 1959, and is very similar to #9-0592 except that the ribbon-curled forms chevrons that deflect downward but its top is almost perfectly bookmatched. The spectacular Standard has just the slightest hint of light reddish-brown left at the top's perimeter. Note, too, that the guitar has original wide frets which begin to occur occasionally in this serial number range, replacing the '58-style, thin fretwire.

Closeup of the 'burst's typical, nickel-plated ABR-1 tune-o-matic bridge with individual, metal saddles and no retainer, the termination of the guitars 24 3/4 inch scale, and the stop tailpiece made from a composite pot metal, like Zamac. *(Outlaw Guitars)*

Nothing floats a 'burst boy's boat like a matched, highly-figured top. Serial number 9-0600, 1959, demonstrates one of the more fascinating aspects of curly maple: its ability to polarize and refract light. Subdued from some angles then on fire when viewed from others, sunburst tops can come alive with undulating waves of curl, making the amount or quality of flame--referred to as "action" -- the sine qua non of a Standard.

Art Atwood's breathtaking serial number **9-0605**, 1959, nicknamed, surprisingly, "Curly Wonder," is a terrific 1959 example of wavy, irregular pinstripe under a near-transparent, light red-brown fade.

A provocative 'burst, serial number **9-0608**, 1959, displays double-white bobbin PAFs. This is just about the time white coils begin to appear in PAF humbuckers but it should be noted that black coils still predominate during the early part of the '59 run. By the time serial number 9-1000 +/- 100 has been reached, double-white bobbin and zebra (black-white) PAFs will predominate and rule until well into 1960. *(Kosta)*

Serial number **9-0633**, 1959, with original double-white coil PAFs. Note the regular, wide ribbon-curl in the guitar's well-matched top. it is very similar to #9-0631's top and indicates that the two maple caps came from the same board of curly maple. *(Tim Matyas)*

Serial number **9-0631**, 1959. The guitar had thin frets. Even though wider fret wire begins to appear at this time, thin frets still predominate during this early run of '59s. An original Bigsby has been removed (see later Bigsby section) and the vibrato's shadow remains on the bottom of the guitar. Note the wide, regular ribbon-curl in the lightly-faded top. *(John Buedel)*

Yuletide tomfoolery: every 'burst boy is dreaming of a white--and zebra--Christmas.
(Tom Wittrock)

Serial number **9-0629**, 1959, displays exquisite, thick, 3-dimensional ribbon-curl in its faded, honey-amber-colored top. Selective receding of the red aniline has caused the figure to become more pronounced as the pigment tends to stick in the curl yielding a more dramatic top than when the guitar left the factory. *(Tom Whittrock)*

Detail of the 'burst's bonnet-style control knobs which began to appear on the Les Paul model in mid '55 and continued on the Standard until mid-'60.

The same guitar resting against a tweed Fender Bassman. Note that the rhythm PAF has been reversed to effect an out-of-phase sound a la Peter Green.

Serial number **9-2204**,Total faded 59 with double white PAF in the lead position.

Gary Moore's Serial Number 9-2227

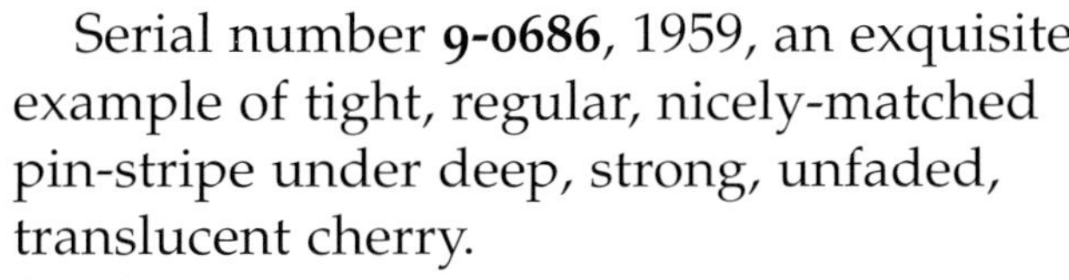

Serial number **9-0686**, 1959, an exquisite example of tight, regular, nicely-matched pin-stripe under deep, strong, unfaded, translucent cherry.
(Kosta)

A complete fading of the red aniline in serial number **9-0644** has left this '59 a glowing amber-yellow over dazzling, pencil-thin stripes. the guitar resembles #9-0636 in curly grain in the top and #9-0646 even more in that the figure on the knob sideis much lighter than on the bass side.

Serial number **9-0646**, 1959, has double-black bobbins and thin frets. note the thin, light, irregular flame with upward deflection on the toggle switch-side, similar in figure to serial number 9-0640 and the poorly-matched, virtually-plain piece of maple on the knob side. The guitar;s top is almost identical to #9-0644 and the two guitars look like twins.

By serial number **9-0653**, 1959 the flitch of pinstripe maple that had been used to construct the tops of more than a dozen sunbursts, from #9-0636 to #9-0652 had begun to run out. Is it possible that planks of the necessary length to make a dozen of so 'bursts at a time where available to Gibson? This 16 serial number range, with its similarity of curly caps, seems to say so. At the very least, many of the guitars made within these numbers came from the same piece of wood.

Consecutive serial numbers with little in common: Albert Molinaro's **#9-0656** has a double-roller, B-7 Bigsby vibrato placed over factory-original, pearloid circles covering the original, factory-drilled, stop tailpiece-mooring holes. The top consists of nicely-matched, fuzzy ribbon-curl and has faded to a warm "honeyburst."

Serial Number **9-0657**, also 1959, has a nicely-matched pin-stripe top with heavy, medullary grain running vertically. The two, consecutive '59's have had their tops constructed from different pieces of maple. Guitars with sequential serial numbers can be remarkably similar or can have nothing in common, arbitrarily and capriciously having had their tops "selected" with almost haphazard concern for appearance. #9-0657's top is either slip-matched -- the piece on the bass side was originally either above or below the toggle switch-side piece of wood on the original plank of maple and moved beside the other half to construct the top -- or has been poorly bookmatched. This casual disregard for the appearance of the company's second-best solidbody indicates a rather desultory orientation towards the model obviously not shared by contemporary devotees.

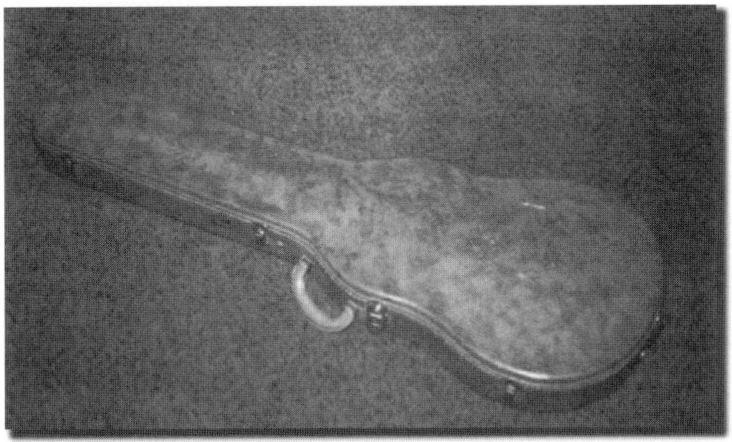

The case associated with a sunburst Les Paul Standard, with mottled, chocolate-brown tolex exterior and posterior fornix-hued, pink, plush interior, didn't come cheap; it cost $42.50. and if you wanted the case cover, it was another 30 bucks.

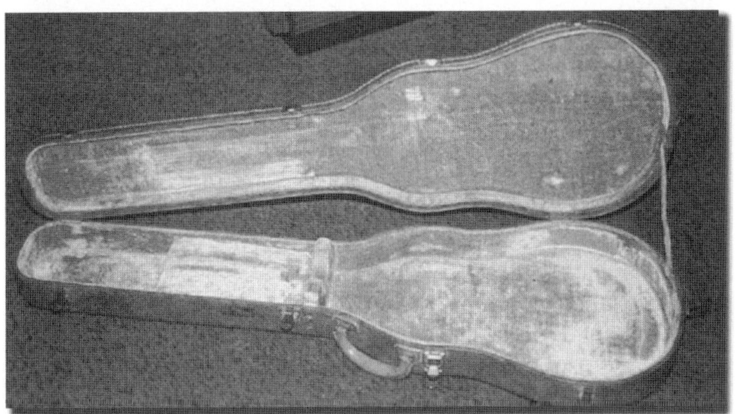

A pristine example, serial number **9-0640**, 1959, displays the refractive quality of flamed maple. Note how the wavy pinstripe-curl on the bottom appears much denser than in the left photo, although the camera angle is only slightly different for each picture. The two shots seem to be of completely different guitars.

A 'burst's typical serial number inked-on in black on the back of the peghead. Notice the space between the year digit "9" and the 4-digit serial number. when more than 9,999 instruments were produced by the company in one year, the space was filled in with a "1". the typical Kluson Deluxe single stripe 9says "Deluxe" in the central, vertical stripe on the tuner's housing), single ring (the little circle between the tuner button and the shaft; double ring Kluson Deluxe tuner begin to appear in late 1960) tuner have tulip-shaped, plastic buttons which have a tendency to deteriorate with age like many plastic, guitar products made during the 40's and 50's.

(Richie Friedman)

Serial number **9-0697**, 1959, has faded finish over thick, regular tigertail-curl. The guitar is well played with a small amount of arm wear but the thick fingers of flame make up for it. Note the clean Fender Bassman. Spectacular, 3-dimensional tops like this one are a sunburst advocate's dream. *(Guitars 'R 'Us)*

An outstanding examples of a bookmatched top, this sunburst serial number **9-0799**, 1959, formally owned by Brad Whitford of Aerosmith. This guitar had a fatal accident and was renecked. Mike Reeder now owns this beauty. This guitar has deep waves of thick, regular ribbon-curl radiating in downward chevrons. few '58-'60 Standards have bookmatched tops.

A sunburst's maple cap is 7/16 to 8/16 of an inch thick at its deepest point. Of the approximately 1700 sunbursts estimated to have been produced, and the estimated 1300 or so extant examples, only 20-25 percent have superbly flamed, matched tops; fewer still have perfectly-bookmatched tops. *(Tim Kummer)*

Serial number **9-0839**, 1959, with its almost-completely-faded and beautiful, nicely-matched, fuzzy-flame top looks a lot like serial number 9-0697. it has a black-white PAF in the front position and resides in the author's collection. The geraniums are factory-optional.

The hottest little appliance to cook on since Hotpoint unveiled its 125 BTU, 6-burner range, Seth Lover's double-coil instrument of aural torture blasted its way to the carved top of goldtop Les Paul Models about mid-1957. earliest versions of Gibson's humbucker had no "Pat. Applied For" sticker on their baseplates and have brushed nickel covers. PAF output varies from 7.0 to 8.5 kohms (Duchossoir says 7.1 to 9.0) with ultimate sustain and timbre, according to many enthusiasts, occurring at about 8.0 Kohms. Of course, gain increases with resistance but, as larry DiMarzio once noted, past a particular resistance, sustain and timbre of the pickup suffer.

Two pictures of serial number **9-0901**, 1959, with double-white-bobbin PAFs, deep, with pencil-thin curl and a beautiful, unfaded but unmatched top. Note how different the guitar looks in each of these photos. When the viewer moves 45 degrees to one side, the flame in different portions of the top light up or disappears almost completely. *(Kosta)*

The Brock -'Burst'

Spectacular top has emphatic, 3-dimensional figure forming downward chevrons. But it's the guitar's translucent, deep-red, almost-burgundy color that makes it incomparible.

The most famous sunburst Les Paul Standard of all, serial number 9-0913, 1959, is seen from several angles, dubbed the Brock 'burst because of its impeccable provenance -- Cheyenne's Brian Brock has been an integral part of the vintage guitar seen for 20 years -- the instrument has attained almost mythic status having graced the cover of successive editions of Tom Wheeler's *American Guitars* (Harper & Row) and has set a standard for beauty against which all other Standards are measured.

The guitar was purportedly obtained from the original owner by Brock in trade for a 1957 Cadillac Biarritz convertible.

The Brock 'Burst and Nacht Worst: the famed Brock sunburst sitting next to serial number **9-1898**, 1959.

This spectacular '59, serial number 9-2020 with its inch-wide swatches of thick, deep ribbon-curl near the pickups, is remarkable similar in top wood and color to the Brock 'burst.

1958-1960 Sunburst Les Paul

A fast hand-vibrato and thick, stinging, single-string, treble runs were hallmarks of the late Paul Kosoff's style, aided and abetted, of course, by the requisite Les Paul Standards. On songs like Free's "All Right Now," Kosoff's preference for a 'burst's treble position becomes apparent.

A '59 with the pickguard removed to display bookmatched.

A '60 with Bigsby removed and fuzzy flame.

A trio of 'bursts from the Gary Winterflood Collection which contains Kosoff's '60 with covers doffed to show off two zebras.

Serial number **9-0934**, 1959, tight, light, pinstripe in a nicely-matched top with strong, cherry color left. Note the double-white-bobbin PAF in the rhythm position and the zebra in the treble.

Serial number **9-0937**, 1959, has a top virtually identical to #9-0934 with light, regular pinstripe.

Fuzzy Flame on the bass side of the top doesn't match the more, regular flame on the knob side of serial number 9-1061. but its pristine condition and strong, translucent, cherry color make for a pretty guitar.
(Mark Quinton)

You'd swear serial number **9-1089**, 1959, nicknamed Ralphie, had a one piece top. But, although not bookmatched, the figure in the two pieces of maple is so well-aligned that it seems to run consistently across the top without stoping at the center seam. Although both vintage guitar guru George Gruhn and author /Gibson exert Andre Duchossoir aver that some one-piece top sunbursts were produced, it is our opinion that no factory-original, genuine one-piece top, three-piece top, or two-piece top with off- center seams were ever reduced by Gibson. Note the 2 double-white-bobbin PAsa under the square-cornered nickel covers. *(Ed Seelig: Tom Wittrock)*

Serial number **9-1094**, 1959, with deep, translucent, burgundy color over a pretty, nicely-matched top; nicknamed "Rusty."

Serial number **9-1108**, 1959, nicknamed "Whitey," obviously because of the two, double-white PAFs, which certainly wouldn't distinguish the guitar from others in this serial number range. It has a beautifully-matched, light pinstripe under the ice tea-color fade.

Unusual, yet attractive, mottled, marble-like figure on the switch side of serial number **9-1165**'s, 1959, top doesn't match the regular, light figure on the knob side. The guitar has covered double-whites.

A considerable amount of mythologizing has developed around white bobbins as used in Patent Applied For humbucking pickups. They begin to appear in 1959 around serial number 9-0600 in limited amounts and by serial number range 9-1000 or 9-1100 had begun to predominate in PAFs. Early in the sunburst's ascendancy as the pre-eminent rock'n'roll guitar, devotees developed a preference for white bobbins (the coil form is white butyrate plastic, never cream-colored), a predilection originally based on appearance alone. As the predisposition for whites evolved, however, players began to hold the opinion that whites actually sounded better than PAFs utilizing black-coil forms, an opinion not supported by any empirical data. Was it wishful thinking? self-delusion?

Randy Klimpert an expert in plastics used in guitar accessories says: "The white color in white bobbins is actually the absence color namely black. I mean, black bobbins get their color from carbon. When the company temporarily ran out of black, carbon pigment in 1959, white bobbins were the result. Now carbon is also used to make resistors which means it has electromagnetic properties."

True, at low volumes -- the volume at which '50's guitar players used to set their amps -- a marginal change in the electrical properties of the pickup would have been inaudible. But through a Marshall isn't it possible that at least a marginal change in timbre might be heard? So, the preference for white-bobbin PAFs might be more than just aesthetic. Note that approximately 5,000 turns of 42-gauge wire are wrapped around each bobbin to a resistance of about 4Kohms per coil for a total of about 8Kohms. PAF resistances vary from about 7.5 Kohms to as much as 9.02 Kohms. Note too that the lead wires on PAFs are always black and that removing the pickup cover slightly increases the output of the pickup particularly on the high end . . . or is this just more sunburst mythology?

Serial number **9-1167**, 1959, shows the same shadow-and-light, marbleized effect in its top as #9-1165. The tops of the 2 guitars were cut from the same plank of maple with the same rather indistinct figure. Number 9-1167 also has double-whites.

Serial number **9-1175**, 1959, with pencil-thin pinstrip on the switch side of the top and multi-directional flame on the other. The guitar has a beautiful, translucent, burgundy-brown fade. The double-whites are original.

1958-1960 Sunburst Les Paul

Serial number **9-1203**, 1959, with light indistinct, mottled figure all over the top. A transparent, light cherry red color remains.
(Mark Quinton)

This unbursted serial number **9-1228**, 1959, has beautiful, regular, wavy flame under a completely-faded, honey-amber finish.
(Tom Wittrock)

A nicely bookmatched top with regular, pencil-thin striping highlights serial number **9-1688**, 1959. Notice the dark rim of residual finish at the bottom of the guitar as through it had stood in s stand that shaded the bottom

Two views of serial number, **9-1838**, 1959, with very light figure in the top. Note the great similarity of top grain to serial number 9-1839, 1959, a Standard with double-whites purchased 20 years ago by the author. These two, sequentially-numbered guitars had their tops fabricated from the same plank of curly maple.

Serial number **9-1839**, 1959: the knob-side piece of maple is identical to both halves of #9-1838's top although the more emphatic figure on the switch side might have come from elsewhere. *(Richie Friedman)*

Tom Keifer's serial number **9-1850**, 1959, has faded to a transparent gray-green akin to the color of light ice-tea. Note the very light figure and the stream of mineral running vertically near the knobs.

Tom Keifer featured in 20th Century Guitar magazine.

Serial number **9-1854**, 1959, with exquisite, 3-dimensional, irregular ribbon-curl under a variegated, translucent, light-burgundy finish.

Serial number 9-1864, 1959: although whites are very common in this serial number range, these are not indigenous to this guitar. No small amount of controversy has arisen regarding the practice of replacing factory-original, black bobbin PAFs with the more comely double-whites or zebras. Traditionalists insist the guitar should remain intact and as pristine as possible and solder joints at the pots should not be broken; others opt for the superior aesthetics (and better timbre?) of whites. *(Kosta)*

Four '59s cluster within six serial numbers present remarkable similar specifications. With the exception of #9-1872, the guitars all have thick, wide, swirly ribbon-curl. The group insinuates that 'bursts, like most models of most manufacturers, were batched, that is, a number of the model were fabricated at the same time -- rather than one at a time -- and numbered sequentially. *(Kosta; Tom Wittrock; Mark Quinton)*

9-1872

9-1873

9-1868

9-1870

Only three left-handed Les Paul Standards with cherry-sunburst finish were produced; two of them are shown here. The guitar on the right with the faded Nehi-orange finish over light, blotchy figure is a '59. The other (below) is a '60 and is currently owned by Paul McCartney. It has o colorful history and in the last decade has ben owned by luminaries like Rick Neilson, George Gruhn, Ed Seelig, Sten Juhl, Tim Kummer and others. Compare the '60 "reflector" knobs with silver discs on top to the '59's typical gold "bonnet" knobs. (Rittor Publishing)

The more '59's from this period with double-white-bobbin PAFs *(Richie Friedman)*

1958-1960 Sunburst Les Paul

This photo of serial number **9-1891**, 1959, display the guitar's nicely-matched pinstripe top. This type of flame, preferred by many sunburst aficionados, is also referred to as fiddle-back maple; others collectors like ribbon-curl. Pinstripe-curl has a tendency to have tight, medullary grain, imparting a kind of grid pattern of intersecting, perpendicular lines to the top. Note 9-1891's typical gold bonnet knobs. By this serial number range the standard. '59-style neck with fatter frets (than '58's and very early '59's) and aslightly less-meaty neck--one that's a bit thinner in the palm--has been achieved

Combined with a propensity to have white coils and nice tops, this part of '59-offers the sunburst buff some of the finest examples of the model. Serial number 9-1887, 1959, has a virtually identical top to #9-1891 except for its completely faded, unburst finish. Note the typical, cream colored, butyrate-plastic pickguard, pickup rings, and switch ring. These plastic parts have developed a market unto themselves, with original cream pickguards and pickup surrounds fetching large sums. Fifteen or 20 years ago, a 'burst could be purchased for the price of a set of pickup rings on today's vintage-parts market.
(Tom Wittrock; Steve Ferruccio)

At right is the exquisite serial number **9-1898**, 1959, appearing with non-original double-whites. Below is serial number **9-1899**, 1959, which has a beautiful, but completely dissimilar top. *(Kosta; Bob Price)*

Sometimes the cream-colored butyrate pickguards on Les Paul Standards discolor a bit because all plastic from this era is somewhat unstable under extremes of heat and humidity. This condition has mildly afflicted this flamey '59 although its pickup rings, made from the same cream-colored plastic, are unchanged in color. These butyrate-plastic pickup surrounds typically have a small oval impressed in their undersides with "M-69" inside. But, hey, what's the deal with the pickup rings on Jeff Beck's 'burst when he played for the Yardbirds? They're black not cream-colored. In fact, some goldtops from 1957 and '58, especially the ones from '57, had black, plastic parts including pickguard. Historian Richard Smith notes that these might have been from the Les Paul Custom of the era and have been appropriated for the goldtop Les Paul model. Another explanation is that Becky might have copped pickup units from an SG Les Paul and dropped the later 'buckers as well as the rings in his 'burst.

Controversy surrounds the discussion regarding the progenitor of the sunburst Les Paul sound. Certainly the model's most visible proponent is Jimmy Page, but Jeff Beck, Eric Clapton and Keith Richard, among others, were running all over the States trying to get an early Les Paul with humbuckers. At the same time Mike Bloomfield was using one of the guitars with the Butterfield Blues Band; Bloomfield is historian George Gruhn's choice as the 'burst's standard bearer, even though an argument could be made that Keith Richard's Bigsby equipped '59 was being used on Stones' tunes at least as early. At one time or another, Mick Taylor, Joe Walsh, Duane Allman, Joe Perry, Brad Whitford and a raft of others have indulged their curly-maple fantasies. But of all the second generation sunburst acolytes, none gets that mid-range crunch con brio like Billy Gibbons do out of Pearly Gates and the Reverend of Tone gets one of the author's votes as the Les Paul Standard's most important disciple. The other author worships Page, however as the true avatar of the sunburst Les Paul Standard whose flame-top hammer of the Gods powered Rock's heaviest band, despite his insistence that fretted instruments can be vowed.

But the final determination as to who is the sunburst Les Paul's chief avatar remains with you, good reader. Who is your favorite 'burst boy?

Publicity photo from Swan Song Records press kit.

9-1923

9-1925

Serial number**9-1925**, 1959, (right) has a virtually identical top to #**9-1923**, (left) nicknamed Donna by owner Tom Wittrock. Not the latter's deep translucent,burgundy finish over thick ribbon-curl extends into the central part of the top to a greater degree than most color-distribution on sunbursts.

1958-1960 Sunburst Les Paul

The absolutely spectacular serial number **9-1878**, 1959, owned by Al Romano. All hint of cherry-red color hasfaded from the top leaving a deep ambertint. The toggle switch-side of the top has outrageously thick, deep, 3-dimensional waves of curl. The dissipation of red aniline is less significant in the flame than in the surrounding wood, yielding an even more dramatic, striping effect than when the guitar was new. #9-1936 had factory-original, double-black-bobbin PAFs. Double-whiteshave been retrofitted, however, raising the question of the advisability of this practice.

Soul Kiss: Ace Frehley's magnificent '59 #9-1878 with its totally-faded finish and breathtaking, thick ribbon-curl. *(Richie Frieman/We Buy Guitar*

Another '59 with nicely-matched, dancing dactyls of rippling flame.

Serial number 9-0597, a '59 with pencil-thin stripes of deep, bookmatched curl under an almost-totally-faded top. The emphatic flame forms tight, downward chevrons in the bottom portion of the maple cap.

Two serial numbers apart, serial number **9-1945** and **9-1947**, 1959, have absolutely no similarity of top wood, having been manufactured from different planks of maple.
(Tim Kummer/Guitar Trader)

9-1945

9-1947

Sunburst mavin and lifelong devotee, Tom Wittrock discusses his specialty with Brooklyn's Lou Gatanas, another 'burst fan.
(C.L. Amalfi)

1958-1960 Sunburst Les Paul

Serial number **9-1953** has double-blacks while serial number **9-1961**, 1959, has double-whites.

9-1961

9-1953

Occasionally a 'burst appears with flame like serial number **9-1974**, 1959, with a stripe of curl every few inches or so. The finish has faded to a transparent, pale cherry at the perimeter of the top.

Wiggly, tight pinstripe graces this unburst's top, serial number **9-1978**, 1959. Note the zebra. *(Gary Winterflood)*

Consecutive serial numbers **9-1980** and **9-1981**, 1959, aptly demonstrate the fascination and enigma associated with sunburst Les Paul Standards. Albery Molinaro of Guitars 'R' Us, devoted sunburst and Korina fanatic elucidates: "Each one is completely different; you never know what you're going to get the first time you open the case. That's part of the charm. Will it be flamed to death... or plain as hell?" *(Wittrock)*

9-1980

9-1981

The Gold Finish was abandoned in 1958 to make way for the beautiful Sunburst Finish

9-2216

9-0656

9-2218

9-0697

9-1959

9-0889

9 0627

9-1982

1958
Serial Number N/A

9-1981

1960
Serial Number N/A

9-0597

9-2314

Marsh

Photo Courtsy of Tom Wittrock Serial # 8-6894

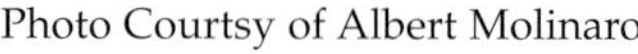
Photo Courtsy of Albert Molinaro

Photo Courtsy of Tom Wittrock Serial # 9-2012

" Same Guitar Different Angle "

Superlative number **9-2012**, 1959, has double-blacks. The wide, deep, irregular ribbon-curl waves under a transparent, amber-tan finish. *(Wittrock)*

The third of only three left handed 'Bursts

1958-1960 Sunburst Les Paul

Serial number **9-1999**, 1959, with and without pickup covers and with and without 1964 Corvette. The guitar has non-original double-whites. Of course, the pickup covers don't have to be unsoldered from the pickup baseplate to determine what color the bobbins are. By removing the whole pickup unit from the instrument by unscrewing the four retaining screws in the pickup ring, both coils can be viewed. For the bobbin with adjustable polepieces, unscrew one of the pole screws; the color of the bobbin can be observed through the polepiece hole. To view the other bobbin, flip the pickup over and remove one of the two brass, inspection screws in the baseplate beneath that bobbin. Although this hole is very small, the white color of a white bobbin can be easily identified. *(Richie Friedman)*

Relatively plain tops on serial numbers **9-2037** and **9-2044**, 1959, although #9-2037 does have a little bit of action on its bass side.

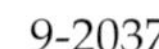

9-2037

9-2044

True grit and Rit: serial number **9-2148**, 1958, once belonged to Lee Ritenour. It has deep but fuzzy striations under an almost-completely-faded finish except, and not commonly, near the toggle and a black-white in the treble position.

Sunburst players prefer a 'burst that weights about 8 pounds total. Even though some 'bursts weighing as much as 9 or 9 1/2 pounds still sound good, the rule of thumb is: the lighter the better. The one-piece, Honduras mahogany body and neck -- a lighter grade of mahogany than the African species that was used by Gibson in the early part of the 20th Century -- can add to a sunburst's featherweight feel.

The perfect 'burst follows the Rule of Eights a featherlight weight of 8 pounds and a resistance in each PAF of 8 Kohms.

Billy Squire gots one

What one 'burst boy referred to as a "cannula in your arm" causes 'burst collectors to continually upgrade their collections, adding better and better examples of the model. A small portion of the author's quixotic collection is shown.

Serial number **9-2180**, 1959, is completely faded but does have pretty, regular, light wavy pinstripe and a zebra in front with a double-white in back. *(Joe Steffanini)*

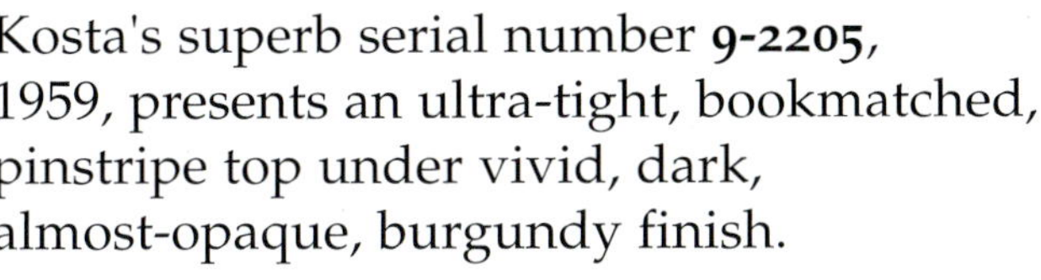

Kosta's superb serial number **9-2205**, 1959, presents an ultra-tight, bookmatched, pinstripe top under vivid, dark, almost-opaque, burgundy finish.

A funny thing happened on the way to the spray booth at various times during 1959: 3-color sunburst finishes on Les Paul Standards. Yes, Cynthia, for whatever reason--perhaps to mimic Fender's 3- color, sunburst finish on Stratocasters--the company began spraying tobacco-brown shader, the same color used to achieve the tobacco-brown finish on ES-335s and ES-345s of the period, on the outermost perimeter of its Standard's curly-maple top. Of course, this begs the obvious question: Did Gibson really make tobacco-sunburst Standards? This is an extremely controversial topic among sunburst experts. George Gruhn avers that tobacco-sunburst Standards were a custom-order option and, once again, since the dark-brown lacquer was being sprayed on the thinline series.

9-0925

9-0926

The first batch of 3-color sunbursts appeared in serial number range 9-0900. Here sequential number **9-0925** (above) and **9-0926** (left), 1959, have double-whites and the latter has a nicely-matched pinstipe top. The 3-tone effect in 9-0925 is much more dramatic however, as much of the original finish is unfaded. The fact that the two guitars have sequential serial numbers and are both tricolors implies that another explanation, other than that they were custom-ordered, may be correct.

Gibson surely sprayed a number of 'bursts with the finish too. Gruhn further offers, however, that the back and sides of these custom-ordered "tobaccobursts" were stained walnut ("Sunburst Gallery", *Guitar Player,* March 1985). However this is not the case as the company used the same finishing procedures on tobacco-sunburst Standards as on its cherry-sunburst finish: the back, sides and neck were sprayed with the same tobacco-brown lacquer as the sunburst on the maple top. When the tobacco color fades on the back of the guitar, it yields a walnut appearance. (See steps and procedures in spraying a sunburst Les Paul Standard finish, the following page).

The dark, tobacco-brown exterior rim of color is unmistakable on this '59. *(Mark Quinton)*

9-2314

9-2342

Three-color sunburst also appears in serial number range 9-2300. These two '59s exhibit an almost-black rim of finish around their perimeters. Number **9-2314** has spectacular, opaque, dark brown over wavey, even flame. Number **9-2342** displays a narrower band of dark, outside color but has a middle layer of unfaded cherry-red. #9-2314's back and sided are dark brown but 9-2342 has cherry-red back, sides and neck. *(Kosta)*

Tobacco Sunburst Finish Exist

So, Les Paul Standards with dark brown tobacco-sunburst finishes exist. When a dark-brown 'burst is encountered, however, the patina may have been achieved in several ways:

1) it was originally sprayed tobacco-brown as a custom-ordered, factory-original, tobacco-sunburst Les Paul Standard.
2) It was an original 3-color, sunburst finish which, over time, has had the red aniline, middle layer fade out as it typically does leaving the appearance of the two-color, tobacco-sunburst finish. Fender Stratocasters from this period display a similar phenomenon, of course; the red component of their 3-color finishes oxidized completely, yielding a brown-to-yellow, 2-color appearance.

3) The 'burst was originally a standard cherry-red finish which, because of environmental factors, has had the red-aniline finish turn to ruddy, reddish-brown which can resemble tobacco-brown.

Another very late-1959 3-color 'burst.
(Mark Quinton)

A light blister-maple top shown through a virtually-opaque, dark brown, nearly-black, tobacco finish. the guitar's finish is identical to an ES-335's from this era. the finish could only have been produced by spraying tobacco-brown, and only tobacco-brown, on the perimeter of the top. the color was not caused by fading or oxidation of cherry-red in the sunburst that has completely faded.

In bright sunlight, this '59 tricolor easily shows off its unmistakable yellow-red-dark brown distribution.

Whereas this '59 with light, mottled figure on the bass side is a cherry-sunburst finish which has faded to a deep, translucent ruddy reddish-brown akin to a dark iced-tea color. *(Jim Morris)*

This faded tobaccoburst is nicknamed Martin. Its dark-brown exterior has become translucent andbeautifully displays the fuzzy waves of curl under it. The back, sides and neck of the guitar appear to be light-walnut brown. *(Kosta)*

Michael Bloomfield is George Gruhn's choice as the player who started the sunburst Les Paul craze although it seems Keith Richard may have been spouting out 'Stones songs well before "East-West" hit in '65. History notwithstanding, this is Bloomfield's '59. It looks similar to the Peter Green-Gary Moore 'burst and has wide, fuzzy fingers of curl under a faded, amber finish except in the area near the toggle switch where considerable faded brown remains. The guitar has an original zebra up front and a double-black in the rear. It has a serious headstock fracture and a splint was employed to firm up the weak wood.

Micheal Bloomfield with his P-90 equipped Gibson Gold Top Les Paul, later to be replaced by a "burst" and a revolution would begin.

Under the able aegis of Dave Deforrest and Tim Kummer, Red Bank, New Jersey's Guitar Trader became the East Coast's foremost vintage guitar store for almost a decade ending in 1987. A savvy combination of superb marketing, unparalleled inventory, excellent location and about a dozen 'bursts on hand at all times made Trader an industry leader. This '59 attests to their legacy.

This '59 has exceedingly-fine pinstripe-curl the width of my grandmother's spaghetti all over the top under a marinara-hued, translucent-finish.
(Gary Winterflood)

From God's hand to us, this flamey '59 serial number **9-0614** belonged to REO Speedwagon's Gary Ritchrath. It kept on rolling to collectors Jaques Mazzoleni, Richie Friedman and Kosta.

If the top of this '59 Standard were the back of a high-grade archtop, there would be no doubt that the company was trying to make a fashion statement. In fact, Akira Tsumura's Citation #14 (*Guitars, The Tsumura Collection*, Kodansha International) which was made in 1974 and appeared on the cover of the mid-'70's Gibson catalog has such a 2-piece back and the artistic intent is obvious. Could it be this the beautiful '59, with heavy flame and so much mineral along the centerseam on the toggle side that it almost looks like spalted maple but only light, unmatched figure on the other, was intended to look this way? That Gibson put so much care into their second-in-line solidbody as to devote this degree of attention to the Standard? That the company took pains to make the model look attractive and felt instead of resignation and apathy a high sense of regard? Nah.

Beautiful thought it may be with its transparent, Nehi Orange-colored finish, no attempt whatsoever has been made to match the two top halves of the maple cap of this '59, reiterating the almost cavalier attitude the company seemed to display toward the Standard.

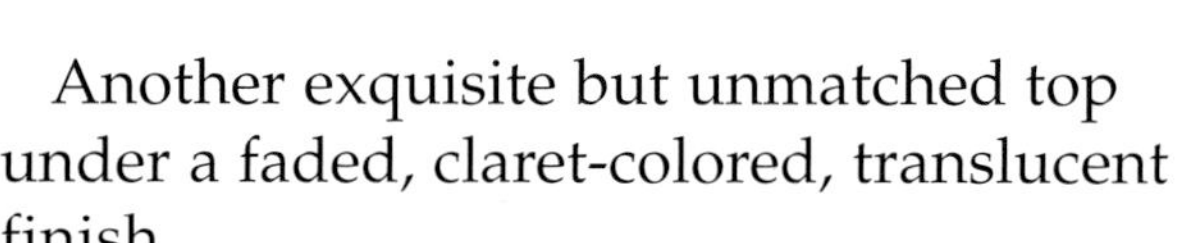

Another exquisite but unmatched top under a faded, claret-colored, translucent finish.

If it ain't got wood it ain't no good

As the ultra-flamey superbursts skyrocketed in value and desirability, the gap between this 20-25% cream-of-the-crop and lightly-flamed or plain-top sunbursts widened. Today Les Paul Standards with unfigured tops have become denizens of the same lower reaches of burstdom as refinished sunbursts. As offensive as predeterminism is to all of us, the caste system of Les Paul Standards is inflexible: the hyper-figured Brahmin 'burst can be significantly modified, have cracked headstocks, be refretted, have Grovers installed, be converted from Bigsby to stop tailpiece yet still bring more money than a pristine but plain-top 'burst. These latter untouchables have been consigned to the category of "players 'bursts", recalling the warning in the Vedas. "If it ain't got wood, it ain't no good."

When Frank Lucido's California Guitar was good, it was very good. This magnificent '59 comes as close to 'burst perfection as its unopened, double-white PAFs, pristine condition, and most of all, its spectacular, bookmatched top under glowing, translucent cherry-red attest.

Two '59s with extraordinary tops. One has wide, fuzzy flame under a bright, cherry-red finish, the other wave after wave of wiggly curl under a transparent, tan fade with just the slightest hint of color.

Another one of those spectacular '59s with deep, 3-dimensional ribbon-curl under a warm, amber fade. Note the emphatic striping near the cutaway where the selective fading has intensified the contrast and thus the figure.

Quartet of '59s with moderate flame

1959

For Your Viewing Pleasure

8-7010

9-0597

Nicknamed Hazel, Tom Wittrock's serial number **9-2324**, 1959, has a strip of arm wear.

9-0629

9-0644

9-0659

9-0669

9-0672

9-0677

9-0692

9-1879

9-1981

9-1843

9-1873

9-1688

9-1946

9-1908

9-0696

9-0823

9-1998

9-2010

9-2011

9-2033

9-2036

9-2020

9-2205

9-2212

0-0133

0-1498

"Pinstripe"

0-0208

A half dozen '59s with light flame or plain tops (Guitar Emporium, Mark Quinton)

"If it ain't got wood, it ain't no good."

Burst

GIBSON

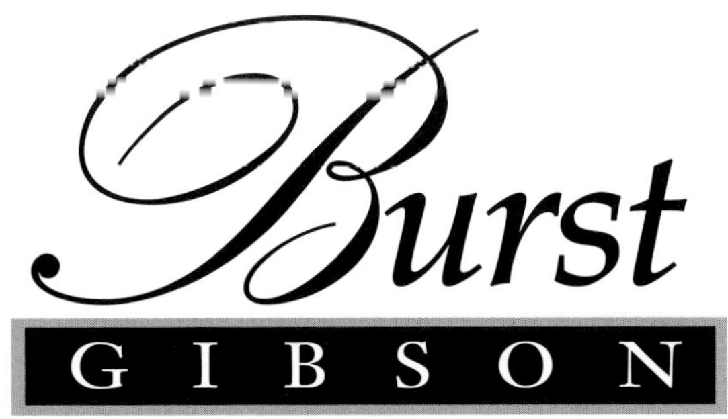

1958-1960 Sunburst Les Paul

Sunburst enthusiasts, take heart, the astronomical price of 'bursts got you down? Note to worry--there may be as many as a few hundreds in the hands of original or second owners. So keep keep hitting those flea markets and garage and estate sales. Richard Broadwell's beautiful photo of a '59 also displays the guitar's shrinking-plastic tuning buttons on the G and B strings, the two tuners most likely to undergo this affliction.

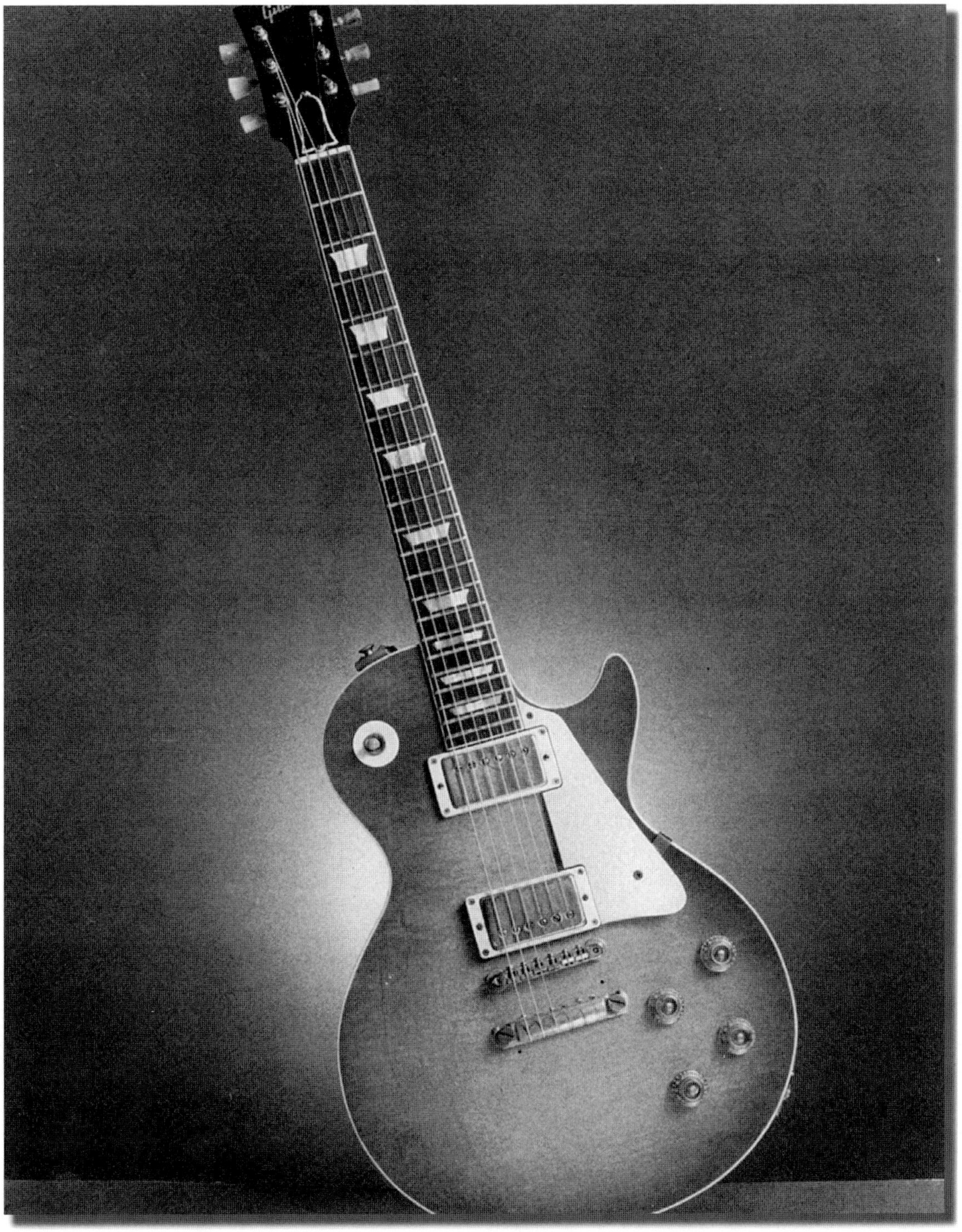

....with Bigsbys

10 to 15 percent of all sunbursts were factory-equipped with an optional Bigsby vibrato at additional cost, almost always a nickel-plated or brushed-aluminum Model B-7, "double roller" model with the spring-pressure bar. The original apparatus is usually removed by contemporary players. Still, a few players like Wally Wachtel choose to leave the whammy where it is.

On a super-flamey Standard like this terrific '59 with a zebra in the rhythm position, conversion to stop tailpiece does not adverseley efect the value...much.

The only hint that this light-iced tea-colored '59 was converted to stop tailpiece is the small square of red remaining near the bottom of the guitar.

One of the first additions to the author's collection with this '59 with original double-whites. Note the Bigsby's shadow near the bottom of the guitar. The conversion to stop tailpiece has the stop bar moored a bit too far back, a rather common condition for stop conversions during the seventies. The guitar appears to have faded to a dark tobaccoburst but was probably a 3-color sunburst finish.
(Tim Matyas)

9-0826

"Preacher"

Tell-tale holes, like snake bite, which are symmetrical on either side of the centerseam, are indicators of a removed Bigsby vibrato. Note also additional screw holes right behind the stop bar's left stud and above the right stud hole between the stop and tune-o-matic bridge.

These two '59s have retained their original B-7s.

Horror of horrors, A '60 with reflector knobs, strong, typical 1960 color....and an original Epiphone solidbody-style vibrato

An unburst from 1959 - almost completely faded and little top action.

"Rocky"

Blood on the tracks of this faded, lightly-flamed, early-1960, serial number **0-0231**

This superlative, early-1960, serial number **0-0208** has wisely not been converted to stop tailpiece: clean, flamey, collectable, Bigsby-equipped guitars should be kept as original as possible.

This '58 is completely faded to light amber-yellow and has a nicely-faded top. Wisely its vibrato has been retained. *(M. Guthrie)*

Serial number **9-0918**, 1959, is just a few serial numbers away from the remarkable Brock-DaPra 'burst, #9-0913, but its top and color are completely different. This pristine, Bigsby-equipped tobaccoburst has tight, regular, wavy pinstripes

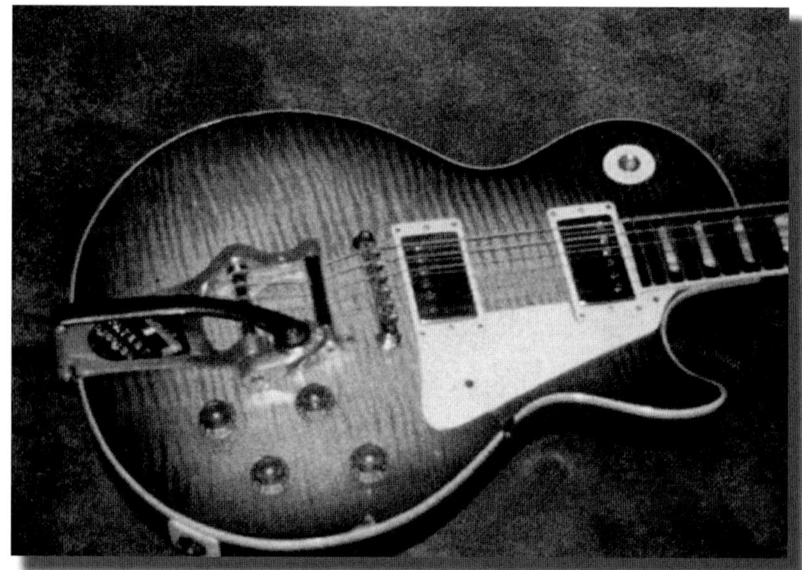

This beautiful '59 has wavy pinstripe under an opaque, very dark brown tobaccoburst finish. One hole is visible behind the left stud hole. the area under the removed Bigsby base is dark tobacco-brown. *(Kosta)*

A '58 with beautiful, wide fuzzy flame, but little figure on the knob side.

Burst
GIBSON

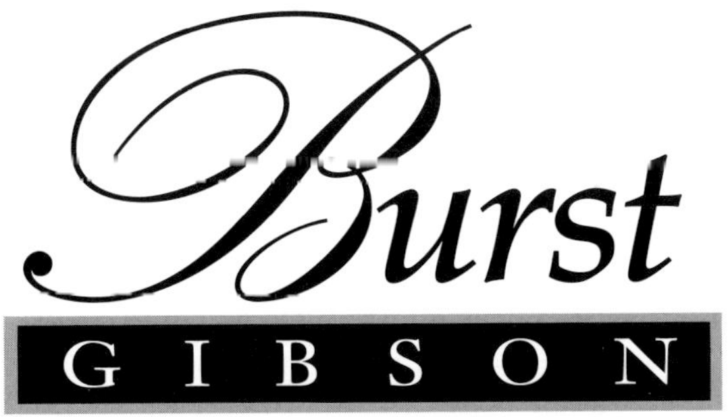

1958-1960 Sunburst Les Paul

"When he was just a kid, his 'bursts were hand-me-downs..."(to the tune of "Rag Doll") A young Mick Taylor took over Brian Jones' rhythm guitar slot . . .and Keith Richard's '59 Bigsby-equipped sunburst when he joined the Stones.

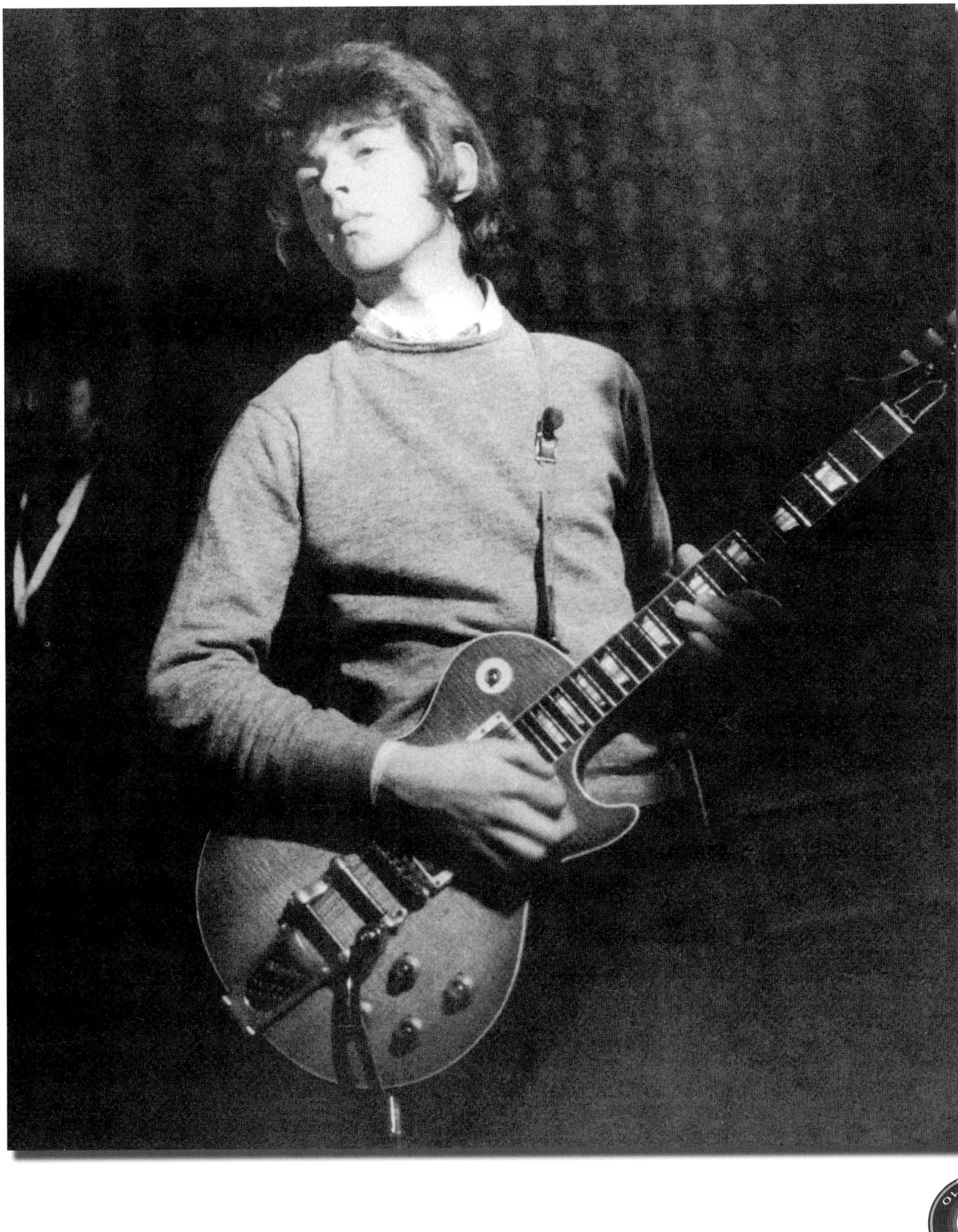

Seven come eleven: dice controls not withstanding, this early-1960 Standard's pretty, transparent, ice-tea fade over equally-attractive, narrow pinstripe and double-white PAF make it to, uh, die for. Have you heard about heaven?

Rick Hoque's '60 has beautiful, deep, cherry color remaining over light, mottled figure. Some residual discoloration remains where the Bigsby's base was. One small screw hole peeps out between the tune-o-matic bridge and the spotail's right stud mooring.

1960's

1960 was the final year for sunburst Les Paul Standard production. Although some of the original series were shipped in early 1961, the original run which began in mid-late 1958 was curtailed at the end of this year. '61's version of the Les Paul Standard was the double-cutaway, SG-shaped guitar, the first few years of which were sprayed all over with the same cherry-red finish used on the sunburst Standard. In addition, the sunburst made its only catalog appearance in Gibson's 1960 brochure and cost $265.00, up about 20 bucks from the model's '58 and '59 price. Furthermore, about 650 'bursts were produced in 1960, approximately the same number as in 1959. (Duchossoir, *Gibson Electrics*, Mediapresse)

Initially, the specifications for 1960's version of the sunburst Les Paul Standard were identical to the Standard produced in 1959. In fact, the cherry-sunburst finishes of '60 burst fade in much the same manner as those of their '59 brethren. However, no later than serial number 0-0700 and probably much earlier -- although sporadically -- Gibson got its red-aniline act together and began spraying an almost-opaque, tomato-soup color, which was much less light-sensitive, on the model. So sunbursts in the serial number range corresponding to the latter half of 1960 rarely fade at all. Moreover, in approximate serial number range 0-1000 to 0-1100 the neck contour was slimmed, yielding a flatter-radiused neck with less wood in the palm. In fact, at the end of the 1960 production run, the neck was slimmed even further to a contour identical to the 1961 SG Les Paul's flat-and-wide specs. While some aficionados prefer this flatter neck for its comfort, the majority opt for '59 meatier contour. There is also sound acoustical reason to believe that the slimmer neck of the '60 sunburst does not refer vibration back into the body with as much amplitude as the heftier '59 neck. The net result is that most 'burst boys don't think the '60 'burst sounds as good as the '59 and for a longtime this opinion was reflected in the '60's slightly lesser desirability and value. Finally, near the end of 1960's production of Standards, white bobbins, which had invisibly powered PAF humbuckers since early 1959, disappear altogether and give way to all-black coils again.

Filled or unfilled screw holes in the top are evidence of a long-gone Bigsby, like on this nondescript '60. Of course, if you looked on the bottom rim of this guitar near the strap button, you'd see filled holes in the mahogany where the hinge of the vibrato was screwed into the guitar.

1960 started out with a bang as the 154th instrument the company made that year is this beautiful serial number **0-0154** which has faded to a transparent, light brown over wide streams of 3-dimensional flame. Note the blank spot without figure above the rear pickup on the toggle side.

Serial number **0-0238**, 1960, has a '59-style neck, two double white coil PAFs and light, mottled figure. The guitar is nicknamed Texas. *(Ron Proler)*

This early '60 serial number **0-0303** is completely faded to a warm honey over light blister maple -- an unburst like many '59's Blister, also known as pock maple, is a variation of birdseye maple and is occasionally mistaken for it. No sunburst Les Paul Standards have birdseye maple tops but blister maple, which features dime-size circles of figure, is occasionally seen on sunburst tops. Bubble maple, also known as quilted maple, presents large swirling circles of figure and was used on 1980's Heritage Elite series of sunburst reissues. Original 1958-60 sunbursts never appear with quilted maple either.

An early ''60, serial number **0-0247**, is very faded like a '59 with white coils rampant *(Mark Quinton)*

These triplets born in 1960 are remarkably similar and within seven serial numbers of each other #0-1483, #0-1484 and #0-1490 have deep, translucent cherry-red remaining over deep swatches of pencil-thin curl. Number 0-1483 and #0-1490 are virtually identical in all respects. The three guitars' tops were certainly cut from the same plank of flamed maple. (Tom Wattrock)

0-1483

0-1484

0-1490

The Patent Applied For Humbucker

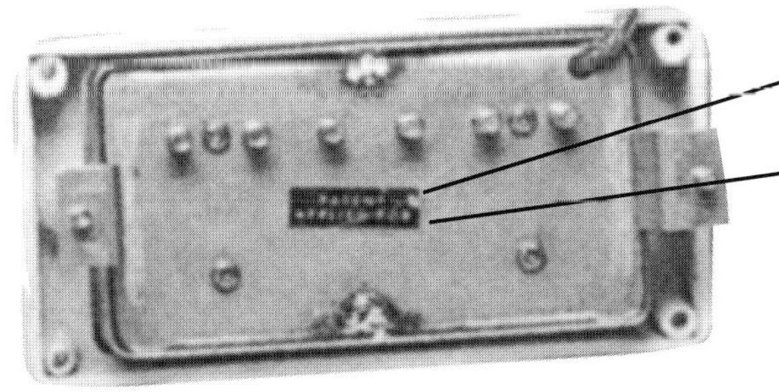

PATFNT
APPLIED FOR

As there is smoke before fire, there was sound before flame and the Seth Lover-designed humbucker pickup gave the 'burst all the sound you could ask for. The first double-coil, hum-cancelling pickup offered by Gibson made it's appearance in the Les Paul while the latter was still a goldtop, replacing the two P-90s in 1957.

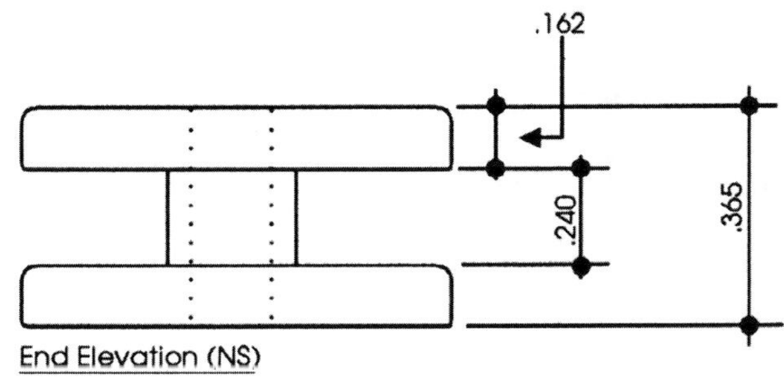

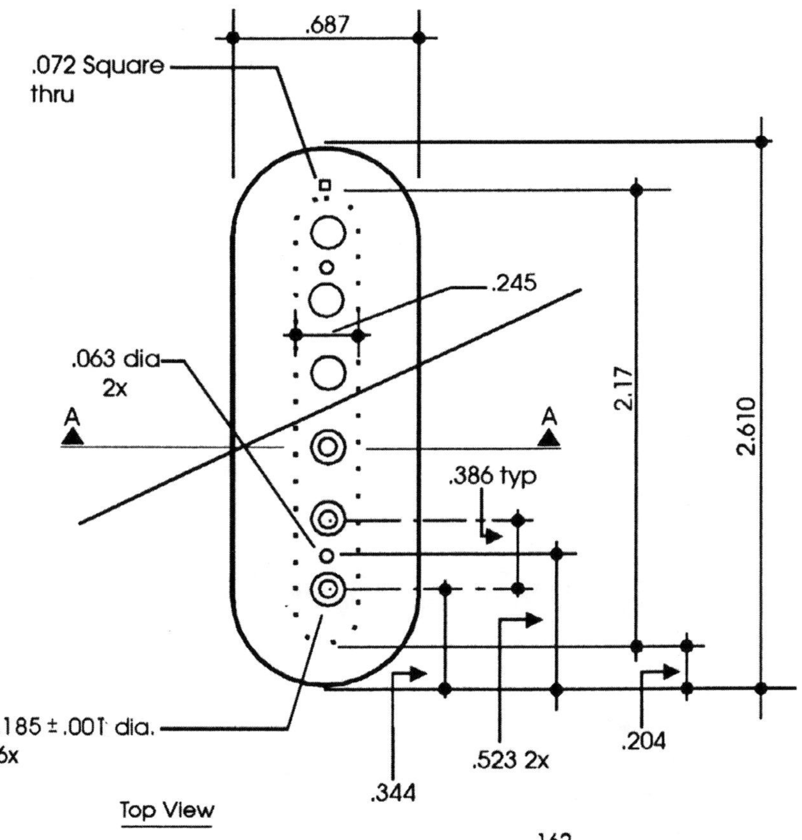

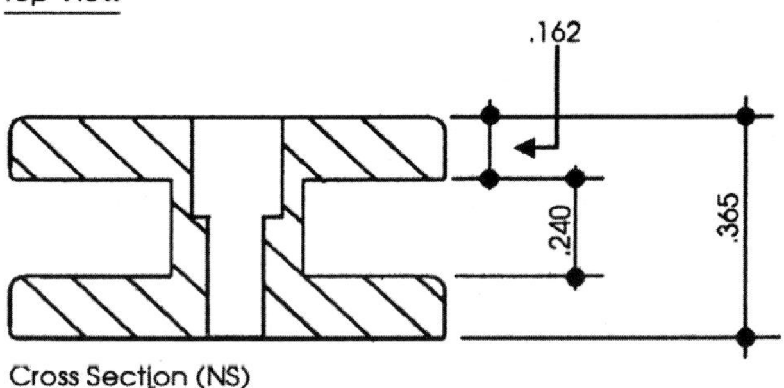

PAF Specs:

Pickup Weight: 119.2 Grams
Adjustable bobbin (south pole) 4.18k ohms
Weight: 22.3 grams
Non-adjustable coil (north pole) 4.1k ohms
Weight: 22 grams

Total turns per bobbin: 5,041 42 plain enamel magnet wire.

Magnet specs:
Weight: 17.9 grams
strength: 20 gauss
dimensions: L - 2.490", W - .492"
T - .120"

Adjustable pole piece:
5/40 Fillister head/slotted machine screw .750" long
Nickel-plated, die point, cold steel, Screw head diameter - .192" Screw total length- .856". Screw diameter (threads) -.120".
Weight - 1.1 grams.

Non-adjustable pole piece:
Stud side of humbucker - nickel-plated
Stud dimensions: L - .479", D - .187"
chamfered corners
Weight: 1.6 grams.

Bobbin mounting screws: Brass, round head Phillips wood screws. Length - .534", head diameter - .154" shaft diameter - .085".

Wood Spacer: Wood - maple. L - 2.218", W - .212", T - .125"

Metal Spacer: Cold drawn steel. L - 2.218", W - .190", T - .125".

Bottom Plate: Stamped nickel silver.

Specifications compiled by Seymour Duncan

A late 50s picture of Seth lover in the Gibson lab. (Courtsey Gibson)

Serial number 0-0271, 1960, is similar to #0-2196 in beautiful figure and faded finish, like a '59.

However, Tom Wittrock's serial number 0-2196, 1960, has gorgeous, thick, 3-dimensional ribbon-curl under an almost-completely-faded, '59-style, transparent tan.

Three 'bursts sitting in an English garden: part of Gary Winterflood's collection. Serial number 0-2192 rests at far left and is seen close up displaying its rear double-white, thick swatches of regular, nicely-matched flame and typical, 1960-style, tomato soup-tinged, cherry-red finish. The guitar was once owned by Gary Granger of Rod Stewart's band.

Gary Winterflood's serial number 0-2164, 1960, blares out its red-yellow color scheme, Note how the deep-red aniline is opaque around the guitars perimeter. On the other hand, the author's serial number 0-2188, 1960, is a warm, honey-amber fade, a la 1959 despite its higher serial number over profuse, dancing curl. This interdigitation of '59-style coloration and 1960's denser hue seems to continue through at least serial number 0-2000.

0-3188

The spirit of Charles Wirz remains with us in Kosta's 1960, nicknamed, appropriately, Phantom. The guitar has light, wavy pinstripe-curl under a '59-style fade which is pale, transparent red-brown. The instrument was indeed formerly owned by the late, legendary Charles Wirz.

Cherry Sunburst

"Gibson used Mobil lacquer from mobil Chemicals to spray their cherry sunburst finishes" says Scott Frielich owner of Buffalo's Top Shelf Music. He's been spraying vintage sunburst finishes for 20 years and offers that Gibson used the same cherry shader to spray the sunburst's cherry-top finish as the cherry-finished back, sides and neck. He also delineated the steps employed to finish a guitar in vintage cherry sunburst a la '58-'60 cherrybursts: 1) spray the whole guitar with clear sealer coat, except the fingerboard 2) pore-fill the back, sides and neckwith mahogany pore filler 3) spray the wholeguitar with another sealer coat 4) spray the whole guitar except the fingerboard with yellow-aniline pigment mixed in clear lacquer 5) spray the back, sides, neck cherry sunburst on the maple top with red-aniline pigment mixed in clear lacquer.

A last look at early '60s with 1959-style specifications. (Mandolin Bros; Kosta)

A striking, early-1960 that strongly resembles the famous Brock 'burst in figure and color a deep, brownish burgundy.

The next five '60s all have 1960's thick, red finish over highly-figured tops. Note that the distribution of the red-yellow sunburst differs somewhat on each of the guitars and that the red is, in fact, somewhat translucent on some of the guitars. All probably fall in the serial number range between 0-3000 and 0-7000 although serial numbers for these guitars are not available. The presence of gold bonnet knobs, instead of reflectors, indicates they were probably manufactured prior to serial number 0-7000. Notice also the continued presence of white coils during this era. *(Ed Seelig; Dan Mills; Gary Winterflood)*

Tight, tight pinstripe -- or fiddleback maple --under a wide, heavy, red finish.

'Burst collectors never die, they just become....Rastafaria: a young Richie Friedman, avec 'fro, and Bob Marley's Al Anderson with 'bursts in the late-'70s.

A spectacular mid-1960, serial number 0-0205 with perfectly bookmatched, thick ribbon-curl forming upward chevrons rest in its flight case. The guitar has bonnet knobs.

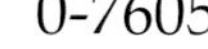

0-7605

This '60 with double-whites has light, irregular pinstripe under a typical '60 finish which is typically faded to translucent pink. *(Richie Frieman)*

Another mid-1960 with heavy, red color over light pinstripe. Note the bonnet knobs.

7000 Series

By the 0-7000 series. Opaque, deep, tomato-soup red usually associated with 1960 sunbursts appears exclusively on the Standard. Apparently, Gibson's crack chemists had figured out an aniline composition that was less likely to fade, less light-fugitive (sensitive) than '58 and '59's brew. Howls from disgruntled Standard owners must have sent Gibson's franchise dealers scurrying back to the company; "What the hell's the story? This guy who's a good customer brings the Standard I sold him last year back to me and the goddamn thing's got no red left in it; it's completely faded out. "As sensitive to their dealers' ministrations as their Standards' sunburst finishes were to sunlight, Gibson got on the stick be mid-'60 and were spraying the new improved cherry-red. Prior to this change in aniline pigment, Gibson issued its "Mr. Dealer" tag (some time in mid-1959) that warned franchised dealers not to put Standards in store windows lest they fade. Once again however the question arises : if Gibson knew from the start that their cherry-sunburst finishes were going to fade and yet chose to market the model that way, how highly could they have regarded the Standard? At approximately the same time the model's gold-plastic bonnet knobs which had appeared on the 'burst since its inception were replaced with reflector knobs, so called because they have chromed, concave discs on their tops. The words "volume" and "tone" are stenciled in black on these discs.

You could go pozzo New Yorker Bob Bozzo's serial number **0-7169**, 1960. The guitar features a typical-'60's, near-opaque, red perimeter with yellow in the center over light pinstripe on the bass side of the top and not much action on the knob side. A double-black and zebra PAF, reflector knobs that say "tone" and "volume" on their silver-chrome centers, Kluson Deluxe tuners with double rings, and a flat neck -- just a bit beefier than an SG Les Paul's -- round out the guitar's specs. Note that the headstock shape, even at this stage of the 1960's production run -- little more than half-way through -- has begun to take on the look of 1961's SG Standard. *(Gill Southworth)*

Gibson

The author's superlative serial number 0-7171, 1960, has broad, isolated thick stripes under heavy red. Note that the double-whites and bonnet knobs are not original to the guitar.

Nicknamed Paula, Tom Wittrock's serial number, 1960, has solid red color, light top-action and bonnet knobs

Serial number, 1960, with fine pinstripe, opaque-red top finish and reflector knobs. *(Wittrock)*

Serial number, 1960 has a mottled, blister-maple, unmatched top with a typical 1960 coloration. Blister or pock-maple tops are quite attractive and rare. Note the reflector knobs.

Serial number, 1960 has a tomato soup-colored, wide distribution over a highly-figured top.

(Mark Quinton)

Absolutely new-looking, right-out- of-the-box-condition serial number **0-7604**,1960 has completely opaque, tomato-soup red over floor flame (if you lay this guitar on the floor and walk around it, you can see the flame). despite its proximity to Gatanas, #0-7606, the guitar has acompletely different top. *(McPeake's Unique Instruments)*

Serial number, 1960: this late-1960 Standard has a translucent red-yellow finish over very light pin-stripe. Note the heavy medullary grain– also referred to as pajama-top grain– near the toggle switch. The guitar has two zebra-coil PAFs and was recently purchased by Eric Johnson. *(Mark Quinton)*

1958-1960 Sunburst Les Paul

Two shots of serial number 0-7606, 1960. They display the guitar's wide, regular, fuzzy flame. Photo courtsey of Lou Gatanas.

On the threshold of eternity, the sunburst Les Paul Standard approached the end of 1960. Its future obviated by a combination of Gibson design engineers' blueprints for a double-cutaway solid body and a contractual debacle with Les Paul, the 'burst was in its death throes at the end of the year and SG body-style Les Paul Standards began to interdigitate with original-series Standards throughout the last 2,000 serial numbers of 1960. Vintage guitar expert Perry Margouleff of New York reports an SG body-style Les Paul Standard as early as serial number 0-8888. However, extant, original series, sunburst bear serial numbers as high as 011495 and 011830 (note that the space between the year digit "0" and the four digit serial number has been filled in with a "1" since more than 9999 instruments were serialized in 1960). This interdigitation of serial numbers for sunbursts and SG Les Pauls is evidenced by the following, very late-1960 production information:

#010001: SG Les Paul
#010180: sunburst
#010838: sunburst
#011169: SG Les Paul
#011189: SG Les Paul
#011495: sunburst
#011830: SG Les Paul

Knight of Shattered Glass: A beautiful '59 protects the author's serial number, 1960, nicknamed Shattered Glass (right). The two guitars have very similartop-figure with extremely wide swatches of ribbon-curl. The '59 on the left, however displays a typical '59 color fade to honey-amber while SG's color remains unfaded, 1960-style deep-red.

Guitar below, Serial number 0-1602, 1960, has moderate flame in both unmatched top halves under a light, ice-tea fade.

Another shot of serial number 0-8600, 60, "Shattered Glass." The guitar is vibrant red. Note that in one photo the guitar has bonnet knobs and in the other it has reflectors; reflectors are correct.

Mark Quinton's beautiful serial number 01145, 1960, was one of the last sunbursts made. The exquisite, tight, deep-pinstripe- curl top has a deep burgundy cast more typical of '59 than '60 and considerably more translucent than '60 finishes. The guitar has double-black-bobbin PAFs which predominate at the end of 1960.

Sunburst Les Paul serial number list compiled by Lou Gatanas.
Email your Gibson serial number to Lou at: mail@unclelou.com

58
8 2023
8 2202
8 3096
8 3688
8 4549
8 5025
8 5148
8 5149
8 5325
8 5346
8 5382
8 5384
8 5385
8 5386
8 5388
8 5395
8 5397
8 5404
8 5413
8 5416
8 5418
8 5419
8 5432
8 5434
8 5438
8 5489
8 5492
8 5495
8 5496
8 5500
8 5502
8 5503
8 5504
8 5512
8 5515
8 5625
8 5660
8 5737
8 5803
8 6192
8 6322
8 6342
8 6397
8 6727
8 6728
8 6730
8 6738
8 6739
8 6742
8 6744
8 6749
8 6750
8 6752
8 6754
8 6761
8 6775
8 6782
8 6784
8 6792
8 6811
8 6900
8 6901
8 6906
8 6912
8 6914
8 6922
8 6927
8 6931
8 7010
8 7042
8 7045
8 7049
59
9 0133
9 0233
9 0279
9 0280
9 0289
9 0290
9 0296
9 0297
9 0299
9 0306
9 0310
9 0313
9 0316
9 0325
9 0330
9 0341
9 0344
9 0347
9 0348
9 0351
9 0352
9 0355
9 0356
9 0357
9 0363
9 0365
9 0367
9 0368
9 0373
9 0377
9 0382
9 0385
9 0387
9 0393
9 0404
9 0426
9 0433
9 0434
9 0535
9 0583
9 0584
9 0592
9 0593
9 0597
9 0598
9 0600
9 0603
9 0605
9 0608
9 0612
9 0613
9 0614
9 0627
9 0628
9 0629
9 0631
9 0632
9 0633
9 0636
9 0637
9 0640
9 0643
9 0644
9 0646
9 0652
9 0653
9 0655
9 0656
9 0657
9 0658
9 0662
9 0663
9 0669
9 0677
9 0681
9 0684
9 0686
9 0692
9 0693
9 0696
9 0697
9 0710
9 0799
9 0823
9 0826
9 0832
9 0837
9 0839
9 0844
9 0848
9 0853
9 0856
9 0871
9 0881
9 0891
9 0896
9 0901
9 0902
9 0903
9 0905
9 0910
9 0911
9 0913
9 0918
9 0919
9 0925
9 0926
9 0930
9 0933
9 0934
9 0937
9 0941
9 0942
9 0943
9 0946
9 0983
9 0987
9 1001
9 1016
9 1061
9 1067
9 1073
9 1081
9 1085
9 1086
9 1088
9 1089
9 1090
9 1091
9 1094
9 1096
9 1103
9 1104
9 1105
9 1108
9 1111
9 1154
9 1156
9 1163
9 1165
9 1167
9 1171
9 1174
9 1175
9 1176
9 1203
9 1227
9 1228
9 1234
9 1235
9 1242
9 1244
9 1250
9 1251
9 1228
9 1303
9 1346
9 1392
9 1511
9 1683
9 1688
9 1703
9 1785
9 1823
9 1838
9 1839
9 1846
9 1850
9 1852
9 1854
9 1861
9 1864
9 1866
9 1868
9 1869
9 1870
9 1872
9 1873
9 1876
9 1878
9 1879
9 1884
9 1885
9 1886
9 1887
9 1891
9 1898
9 1899
9 1901
9 1907
9 1908
9 1913
9 1914
9 1918
9 1921
9 1923
9 1924
9 1925
9 1927
9 1936
9 1942
9 1945
9 1947
9 1952
9 1953
9 1955
9 1960
9 1961
9 1962
9 1964
9 1967
9 1970
9 1972
9 1974
9 1978
9 1980
9 1981
9 1982
9 1984
9 1986
9 1993
9 1994
9 1997
9 1998
9 1999
9 2003
9 2010
9 2011
9 2012
9 2015
9 2020
9 2023
9 2024
9 2035
9 2036
9 2037
9 2044
9 2071
9 2074
9 2077
9 2146
9 2148
9 2173
9 2174
9 2180
9 2188
9 2192
9 2193
9 2195
9 2203
9 2204
9 2205
9 2207
9 2210
9 2212
9 2214
9 2217
9 2218
9 2220
9 2225
9 2227
9 2229
9 2308
9 2311
9 2312
9 2314
9 2317
9 2318
9 2324
9 2335
9 2339
9 2342
9 2498
9 3012
9 5246
951067
60
0 0117
0 0122
0 0133
0 0154
0 0162
0 0205
0 0206
0 0208
0 0231
0 0233
0 0238
0 0247
0 0253
0 0256
0 0257
0 0264
0 0266
0 0271
0 0273
0 0288
0 0289
0 0290
0 0297
0 0302
0 0303
0 0304
0 0308
0 0309
0 0436
0 0599
0 0608
0 0700
0 0718
0 1065
0 1183
0 1193
0 1194
0 1483
0 1484
0 1490
0 1494
0 1495
0 1498
0 1499
0 1502
0 1504
0 1506
0 1513
0 1602
0 1922
0 1926
0 1930
0 1940
0 1943
0 1951
0 1957
0 2031
0 2036
0 2160
0 2164
0 2167
0 2169
0 2171
0 2177
0 2183
0 2187
0 2188
0 2192
0 2196
0 3187
0 3188
0 4973
0 7157
0 7158
0 7169
0 7170
0 7171
0 7180
0 7181
0 7183
0 7275
0 7444
0 7446
0 7448
0 7450
0 7451
0 7452
0 7512
0 7587
0 7592
0 7598
0 7600
0 7601
0 7603
0 7604
0 7605
0 7606
0 7615
0 7623
0 7632
0 7812
0 7935
0 8039
0 8067
0 8069
0 8080
0 8084
0 8087
0 8091
0 8138
0 8145
0 8146
0 8148
0 8152
0 8160
0 8163
0 8164
0 8166
0 8185
0 8291
0 8292
0 8353
0 8354
0 8393
0 8600
0 9254
0 9353
010180
010838
011188
011495